Is There Life After Housework?

2nd Edition

Is There Life After Housework?

2nd Edition

A revolutionary approach
to cutting your cleaning time 75%

Don Aslett

America's #1 Cleaning Expert

Adams Media
Avon, Massachusetts

Published by
Adams Media, an F+W Publications Company
57 Littlefield Street, Avon, MA 02322. U.S.A.
www.adamsmedia.com

ISBN: 1-59337-506-9

Printed in Canada.

J   I   H   G   F   E   D   C   B   A

Library of Congress Cataloging-in-Publication Data
Aslett, Don Is there life after housework? / by Don Aslett.-- 2nd ed.
p. cm.
ISBN 1-59337-506-9
1. House cleaning. I. Title.
TX324.A75825 2005
648'.5--dc22
2005016010

This publication is designed to provide accurate and authoritative information with regard to the subject matter covered. It is sold with the understanding
that the publisher is not engaged in rendering legal, accounting, or other professional advice. If legal advice or other expert assistance is required, the services
of a competent professional person should be sought.
—From a *Declaration of Principles* jointly adopted by a
Committee of the American Bar Association and a
Committee of Publishers and Associations

Many of the designations used by manufacturers and sellers to distinguish their products are claimed as trademarks. Where those designations appear in this book and Adams
Media was aware of a trademark claim, the designations have been printed with initial
capital letters.

Interior cartoon illustrations by jimhunt.us
Interior technical illustrations by Michelle Dorenkamp

This book is available at quantity discounts for bulk purchases.
For information, call 1-800-872-5627.

Contents

Introduction:
Still Looking for Life After Housework?

You are entitled to a life of love, fulfillment, and accomplishment, but these rewards are almost impossible to obtain if you spend your life thrashing and flailing in a muddle of housework. Time—the time to love, to be, and to grow—is the most precious commodity on earth. No one's time should be wasted cleaning needlessly or inefficiently.

Is housework getting old? Not if you keep it young! Making housework go faster and making it more fun were my goals when I started my professional cleaning career as a college freshman at nineteen. Now, after fifty straight years with my hand on the mop and chasing the dust bunnies, I've lived to see these goals fulfilled. I've been able to help many of you cut your time spent cleaning from five years of your life to three years or less. This new edition of my best-known cleaning book gives you the advantage of a half-century of pro cleaning experience. Armed with *Is There Life After Housework?, 2nd edition*, you're going to cut down cleaning to a single year of your life—and you'll enjoy it more, too!

The first edition of this book in 1980 was an instant bestseller. It was the first book to offer genuine professional cleaning know-how and timesaving solutions, and the first ever to bring the professional approach to the home scene. *Is There Life After Housework?* has endured because it really answers the question in the title. If you do housework the professional way, you can get it done faster, better, and cheaper— and you will indeed find that there *is* life after housework.

It's been twenty-five years since this book first saw print, and my once-little college housecleaning business is now a nationwide corporation that employs thousands and takes care of more than 400,000,000 square feet of building space every day. Most of the cleaning principles I recommend now are the same, but new home surfaces, new techniques, and new equipment have also been added to reflect the new home situations today. I've freshened and improved this cleaning classic for today's homes. (And yes, I still work on the job of cleaning every day—it's still not only my life, but my favorite entertainment!)

Happy Cleaning,

Don Aslett

Chapter One
A Clean House . . .
How Does Everyone Else Do It?

Some lie.
Some have mighty lumpy rugs.
Some hire someone else to do it.
Some use only one room in the house.
Some never let anyone in.

Most of us don't use any of these methods to clean our houses. We represent the 95 percent of home cleaners who wonder, often in a state of cobweb confusion, "Just how does everyone else do it?" How do they manage to keep a house clean in the midst of everything else we have to do today?

Newspaper columnists, magazines writers, and celebrity home decorators have tried to provide all the answers for a "perfect home"—and they have convinced too many of us that we don't have a chance. Every time we see another "everything-clean-and-organized" success story, we end up depressed and frustrated. It doesn't make us feel any better to see commercial exaggerations of how well cleaning products work, especially when they're applied to a house in which everything is already perfect. You're not alone in feeling outclassed by the TV commercials featuring an attractive home cleaner wearing designer jeans while she mops the floor with Magic Glow. Occasionally, an immaculate kid or two tiptoes past or a well-groomed dog ambles through the place, after which the "super-smelling clean-all," applied effortlessly, takes over.

We try the miracle formulas, quick tips, and super systems, but when we find ourselves still not progressing in the war against household grime, grit, and grubbies, we wonder why these methods and products seem to work so well for others. "Something is surely wrong with me!" you conclude. "Why am I the only one failing?" When you're doing your best but see yourself falling short of your goals, it's hard to have a bright outlook or a sense of accomplishment.

There's nothing wrong with you or with anyone else struggling to run a home, hold down a job, raise kids, go back to school, and do volunteer work. Housework is never-ending and little appreciated. There are no "super home cleaners." Most people are barely managing to deal with daily crises and demands, just like you are, and they too are wondering what's wrong with them. It's amazing that no real training is provided today for the job few of us can escape: housecleaning. **I can assure you that there are proven ways to have a clean house—and they don't hinge on magic, good luck, or genies in a cleaner jug.** By learning how to *prevent* housework, and by using *professional* cleaning methods, you can reduce your household chore time by as much as 75 percent. You'll simply learn to clean more efficiently and effectively. My confidence in this statement is anchored in more than fifty years as a professional housecleaner—and teaching and listening to thousands of people around the world talk about cleaning.

A Housecleaner is Born

Fresh off the farm and unappreciative of my mother's labors to provide me with hearty meals, ironed shirts, and a clean bed, I found college life a far cry from my comfortable home. My appreciation for that home and for my mother became keener when I discovered how much time and money it took to support myself. To help pay my way, I landed my first nonfarm job, bottling pop for seventy-five cents an hour. The funds left after deductions were not going to be enough to get me through college, so I looked for a better-paying part-time job.

Cleaning yards and houses seemed the best prospect, and so my career as a world-renowned housecleaner was launched. After afternoon classes, I'd suit up in a white uniform and knock on doors, asking if I could assume some of the household drudgery. I received only a few sneers before I was snatched from the street and given a furnace-cleaning job, followed later by some floor cleaning, and then some window cleaning. Next came wallpaper cleaning, wall washing, and cupboard cleaning. On every job, the homemaker would watch and direct as I'd scrub, shovel, and polish. Word got out that an eager housecleaner was loose in the neighborhood, and soon I had more work than I could handle. I hired help, taught them what the homemakers had taught me, and the business grew. Carpet and upholstery cleaning were added to my list of skills. Soon my business was a large one, in demand in towns outside the college city of Pocatello, Idaho.

Over the next ten years my unique housecleaning business received much public recognition—"College Boy Makes Good." Between newspaper headlines I acquired a vast amount of further experience in housecleaning. I also ruined grand piano tops, toppled china cabinets, broke windows, streaked walls, ruined murals, shrank wall-to-wall carpets into throw rugs, and pulled scores of other goofs. But with each job I got better, faster, and more efficient (at cleaning, not breaking). I cleaned log cabins with dirt floors and the plushest mansions around. Some days with five housecleaning crews in operation, we'd clean several three-story homes from top to bottom.

Cleaning skills weren't the only talents needed to run the company; organization was important as well. All of us working in the business were full-time students, active in school, church, and civic affairs, and we had large families. Because my coworkers and I had no alternative, we *had* to develop efficient methods to clean houses.

Many years of experience make me confident that I can show you how to attain greater housecleaning efficiency. Although I now serve as a consultant on building maintenance for some of the world's largest companies, I know that home cleaners face some of the most difficult cleaning problems of all. In preparing this book I've tried to keep in mind the hundreds of other jobs home cleaners must perform simultaneously with housecleaning. Laundry, grocery shopping, cooking, family maintenance, and errands *ad infinitum* will always be required too, as well as the many things we often have to do to meet our professional and social obligations. Though housework can be shortened, and there *is* life after housework, life *during* housework must also go on.

This is why rigid cleaning methods and plans seldom work. Schedules and demands are different in every household, big houses are proportionately easier to clean than small ones, and new houses easier than old (this is why trying to pattern your life after others eventually leaves you disillusioned).

The Key to Freeing Yourself from Housework

Miracle formulas, tricks, and gimmicks aren't the answer, but don't let that get you down, because there is a key to freedom from housework. The first principle of effective housework is not to have to do it! Being able to clean well is great, but it's greater not to have to do it at all. Your real goal is to eliminate all that you can. In this book, you'll learn how to get rid of a lot of it, and take care of the rest quickly and efficiently.

There are "have-to" jobs, no matter how good we are, such as dealing with bathtub rings, cleaning floors, cleaning the toilet, taking out the trash, etc. You'll never escape them. But when you learn to minimize the time you spend on the have-to jobs, you'll finally be able to get to the more progressive projects you've long been waiting to get to, and they'll both become more pleasant!

There is life after housework—and if you do it right,
there can even be life during housework.

Once you start finding the extra time that once was all spent on housework, nothing in your home will be mediocre or dull. You'll rip down anything that's faded or ugly and replace it with the sharpest, most colorful, most refreshing, easy-to-clean things you can find. You'll throw out or sell things that don't fit in. Once you have time, you'll be inspired to repair and refinish. If something is torn or worn or forlorn, you'll look forward to taking care of it, not as a chore, but as a chance to improve some part or corner of the house. The real struggle before wasn't the chore or item you had to service—it was the hopeless feeling that there was never any time for it. A lot of little things that need to be done aren't really much work once you can get to them—and once you actually believe that you *can* get to them, you'll start looking forward to them! That's life *during* housework!

As for worrying about how other people do it, you'll discover that 90 percent of the time you're overestimating their results. Not many others are more efficient nor do they have neater homes than yours. By following the simple secrets in this book, you'll become even more efficient, and you will have more time to enjoy life after housework.

But Aren't Things Different Now?

We look out the windows of our nicer-than-ever homes today onto more traffic, and some of the technology developed in recent years to help us clean and run our homes is astounding. But we still somehow have too much housework to do. The increased efficiency we might have expected from new tools and technology has been offset by the demands of much larger homes with more "stuff" (furnishings, decorations, possessions of all kinds) than ever in them. We all have much more demanding schedules, too. We have faster, better, and quieter automatic washers but bigger mounds of clothes to wash. Despite the self-cleaning oven and maybe a dishwasher, too, the kitchen is forever dirty. The family room has every electronic plaything or entertainment device available but it needs dusting and decluttering badly and there are taco chips on the floor. Our lawns that used to take an hour to mow now take two hours or more (even with much fancier mowers) because we have more grass to mow. Not long ago few houses had garages; now three-car garages are common—with the three cars parked outside because the garage is full of nifty things from inflatable beds to recreation gear that we are desperately trying to get through our housework to find time to use.

Bottom line: Cleaning and home care has not gone away in our new day. Our homes, cleverly designed, built, insulated, and decorated as they might be, are still too often taking more than they are giving. The need for cleaning and maintaining our homes seems to take precedence over the relaxing, heart-warming, and creative activities we hoped to be doing in them. And although home care today seems just as formidable as when I first put pen to paper, now most family members have even less time to do it than we did two decades ago. So we have the same squeeze, the same concern, the same need as we have always had—trying to get all of our home duties done so we can get on to some of the things we *want* to do. Yes, self and home care *is* part of life, but somehow the "life" we think of first is usually things that will expand and delight as well as serve us.

> The professional cleaning approach won't take cleaning away entirely, but it will give you a lot of extra hours. The time rewards of efficient cleaning are real, and the busier you are, the more you'll appreciate them.

Home care is still a big part of life, and it can be a drain and a stressor if we allow it. It is still a struggle to try and get it all done, and to pay for it all. The good news is that there are some better products out there and we are learning to use them better. We are also starting to not only find, but *demand* help on the home front, and we are starting to understand that we need to reduce the clutter that takes about 40 percent of our cleaning and care time. We are also learning more about how to act preventively, so there are some compensators. Above all, we still need to learn how to clean faster. Fast cleaning is just as valid and available as fast food, and it's much healthier for sure. Here is a chance to feast on it!

Chapter Two

Is It Organization . . . or Your Energy Level?

"I get the feeling at the end of every day that I haven't gotten anywhere and I'm never going to get anywhere. . . ." This is how a young mother with a new job, new house, and four small children concisely summed up a basic problem of home care: understanding what needs to be done but feeling that you lack the skill or direction to accomplish it. Even if you know what the rewards will be, constantly thinking you aren't getting there will discourage you and eventually prevent you from wanting to get there.

The Big Magic Word

A big magic word for all of us today is "organization." We think if we could just get ourselves properly organized, we could do anything. So, we spend a great deal of time trying to organize ourselves like the superwoman and superman formulas say we should, but still we seem to get little accomplished. We subconsciously figure the "organizing" is going to do it for us. This is wrong. No organization plan can supply the whole answer or do the work. But there is hope—read on!

There Is No Single Best Way to Organize

Organization is an ever-changing process—it's a journey, not a destination. There are all kinds of ways to organize, and every minute of every day a new approach is thought up. Everyone is different in temperament, attitude, build, energy, and ambition; different situations may require a different style of organization to get the job done. The secret isn't in how you get organized—it's in wanting to be organized and committing yourself to it. Once you are committed, everything will fall into place. You can organize as well as anyone if you really want to or if you have to.

There isn't any official way to organize. You don't have to eat soup first or second in a meal—you can eat it last! Your system of organization should fit you personally. It should be tailored to your style, your schedule, and your motivation. Some of us are day people; some of us do everything at night. *You*—not the clock or calendar—run your life.

Many people think that organization means restriction and limits, but nothing could be further from the truth. Organization sets us free, and it gives us peace, order, and a sense of purpose so that we can get eight hours' work done in three, or so that all our chores are done in bits and snatches of time, rather than a three-hour stint on Saturday!

You don't need expensive files and containers and day planners to organize. If you need equipment, you can make good use of things like inexpensive plastic tubs and cardboard boxes. Once you're organized, cleaning will be much less discouraging.

Some Organizational Myths

Everyone can be organized if we would just quit trying to follow "know-it-all" methods and formulas.

Some efficiency experts, for example, offer this "fool-proof" method of accomplishment: "Sit yourself down and make a list of the things you want to get done. Put the most important ones first. When you get up in the morning, start on the first one and don't leave it or go to the next one until the first is finished. Then go on to the second one, and so on, until you've finished with the list." How could anyone succeed following that kind of organizational concept? It's grossly inefficient, inflexible, and uncreative—not to mention no fun. For years I've worked closely with top executives from many of the world's largest corporations, and I've never met one who worked this way. Yet many ordinary people try desperately to carry out this ridiculous organizational concept, and they suffer endless frustration because they can't make it work. If I followed that style of organization in my business or personal activities, I'd be twenty years behind!

Still not convinced? Look where trying to follow the one-two-three style of getting things done can lead you. Let's say you make a list of the following things to do this week (in addition to your regular chores):

1. Make the kids a birdhouse.
2. Water the garden.
3. Memorize speech for my brother's wedding.
4. Send Grandmother a birthday card.
5. Fertilize and replant those bare patches on the lawn.

You enthusiastically tackle the five projects in the down-the-list style outlined by the efficiency experts. While in town, you pick up the birdhouse materials, and you get started on the birdhouse with full gusto. But you forgot to get a hole saw to make the hole in the front of the birdhouse, so you're stopped at a critical point. The one-two-three track compels you to leave the task and take time out to secure the needed tool, which you do at a cost of two hours of searching and twenty-three miles of driving. You then paint an undercoat on the birdhouse, wait a day for it to dry, and then put on the second coat. After two days, task number one is at last finished, so out to the garden next. You turn on the sprinkler. Four hours later the garden is well watered, and task number two is finished. Next you go into the house for an hour or two to memorize your wedding remarks, numbered three on the list. You then run to the store to pick up item number four, Grandmother's card. You bring it home, sign and address it, and take it to the post office. To put a hero's touch on number five, you pick up a book on lawns, work on the lawn over the last three days, and are finished with all your projects in one week!

Efficiency experts might have a week to spend on all this, but you don't and neither do I. The tasks could easily be done in a day or two with a little margin for daydreaming on the side. How? By relying on your creativity and using a more flexible system. While waiting for the clerk at the lumberyard to round up the birdhouse materials, chat with one of the staff about lawns and at this time get the fertilizer, mulch, and seed for the anticipated patching.

On the way home, turn off the CD player and start to memorize your wedding speech. Once you get home, lay out the materials for the birdhouse and build it. You forgot the saw? No problem! Stop the birdhouse immediately and go turn on the water for the garden, taking your wedding script with you to memorize while waiting for the sprinkler to wet down all the rows. Once the water is going, planting some grass seed is the next order of business. Next, phone your brother-in-law and ask him to send his hole saw home with your child, who'll be coming by in a while from school. Continue to work on the lawn until you're too tired to hustle. Take a breather to write out Grandmother's card so the children can take it to the mailbox on their way to school tomorrow morning. When your child arrives with the saw, drill the hole and paint the birdhouse. By this time, you're rested, so you tackle the lawn again. When you've finished with the lawn, you come in and give the birdhouse a second coat (you were smart enough to buy a fast-drying primer). By then it's late, but there's just enough time to finish memorizing for the wedding. Now all five things are completed in *one* day instead of a week, and look at the time you have left for yourself.

Think this is impossible? It's not.

The way some people cook is a prime example of doing things the most efficient way. I watched my grandmother, who had fifteen children, prepare eight different dishes for twelve people in just minutes. It wasn't a miracle—just good organization and the multiple-track system. No sense waiting for water to boil, biscuits to rise, salads to cool, butter to melt. She simply used the waiting time productively. You've done things like this, haven't you, when you had to?

I watched a one-track-system mother with one small child crumple in total frustration just trying to manage her baby. Five years (and three more children) later, she was doing a marvelous job. How? She learned the four-or-five-track organization system and applied it!

Your mind is capable of it and your body is, too. The success of this system is amazing, and once you get it down, you'll benefit from it in every area of your life.

A large percentage of our housecleaning time is spent "putting out brush fires," as it's called in business—spending three days hunting for your dog because you didn't take three seconds to close the gate behind you. Many of us fail because all our efforts are spent taking care of problems that a little timely action would have prevented. We spend twenty hours a year (and a lot of mental anguish) trying to remove felt-tip marker writing from walls, instead of a minute putting the pens out of reach of the kids; ten hours a year cleaning ovens or stovetops instead of fifteen minutes choosing a pot or pan that won't boil or slop over!

You can apply the multitrack principle to housework, too. In housework, if you wait until one thing is completed before you start another (the single-track system), you'll take forever to finish and you'll never get around to enjoying life. Once you train yourself to the multiple-track method, thinking will be effortless. You'll just roll along accomplishing things. You won't have to drain your think tank or worry or sweat to organize. It will come naturally.

The multiple-track system is the right way to run many projects at the same time—and it's easy if you alternate starting and finishing times. The start and finish of a job are the difficult parts. So start the first project at once! As it gets rolling, begin the second. As the second gets in gear, attack the third. By then the second one is done, so pounce on the fourth, fifth, and sixth; and if the third isn't done, start on the seventh. Here are the secrets:

- Don't start and finish any two tasks at the same time.
- Start another project while you're in the middle of three or four, but don't start one while you're finishing up another project.

Simplicity Versus Procrastination

A great deal of effort is expended as a result of failure to put forth a simple timely effort. Here's a common everyday example: doing the dishes later instead of right after the meal. Notice how a simple chore multiplies itself into a mountain of negative feelings and ambition-destroying discouragement.

Do you take the time, over and over, to cope with an unsatisfactory situation instead of correcting the underlying problem? For example, do you have to adjust the faucet handle just right when you turn it off so the drip is minimized? Or angle and massage that sticky drawer for thirty seconds to get it to slide back in? Or wonder and experiment every time a breaker blows—which one is the lights, which is the heater, which is the outlet, which is the . . . You know what I mean. (See the checklist at the end of Chapter 8.)

The best "organization" is simply deciding to do things before they get out of hand and dictate to *you* how and when they'll be done. **Procrastination never makes things simpler.** Do you clean up and put away things as soon as you're finished (simplicity), or do you throw them in a pile to rummage through as you need them (procrastination)? Do you iron your shirt well ahead of the appointment, or five tense minutes before you have to dash out the door? (And, of course, then you have to take out and set up the ironing board for just one piece of clothing—and you risk scorching the shirt in your haste and having to find and iron another.) Do you make your bed when you jump out (simplicity) or just before you go to bed again at night (procrastination)?

Do you fill out that committee report when it's still fresh in your mind and will take only a few minutes, or do it when it's overdue? You've been strongly reminded to get it in, and now you'll spend hours doing so, because by now you've forgotten facts, mislaid your notes, and had to write an excuse e-mail.

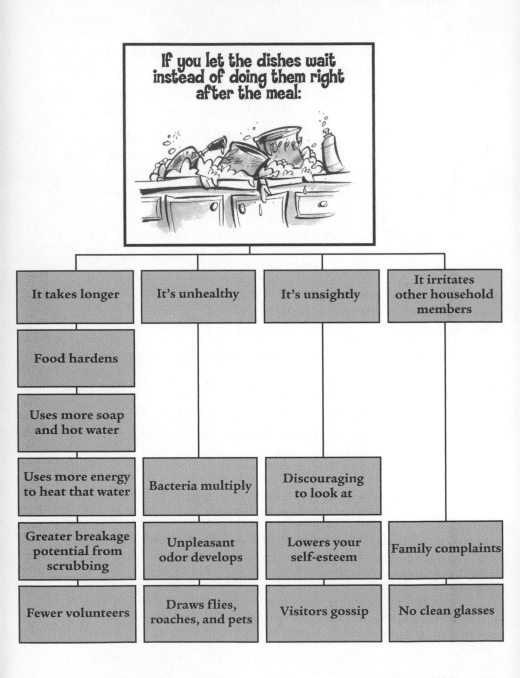

Back to the Ever-Growing To-Do List

We all have our lists of things to do. (I'd be lost without mine!) We don't always do the things on the list, but they're always jotted down. At one point, my list grew to seventy-six "immediate" things to be done. It took all my time just to transfer the list to a new piece of paper when the old one wore out. If your list follows the typical pattern, at the bottom are the hard, unpleasant tasks, such as:

19. Clean the oven.
20. Clean out the garage.
21. Volunteer to baby-sit that annoying neighbor kid.
22. Kick cousin Jack out of the front room.
23. Go through 700 old issues of *Good Housekeeping*.

Or . . .

38. Tell Grant he's not going to get a good review this quarter.
39. Face the banker and get the loan.
40. Get my wisdom teeth pulled.
41. Speak to Justine about finding a better brand of deodorant.

We have to be careful with that villain list. We're often so proud of ourselves for even writing something down on our list that we immediately relax. We say to ourselves, "Boy, I'm glad I got that one started." After a few days we suddenly realize that nothing has been done, and we sneak a look at the list to see if that item has disappeared. It hasn't. We're so relieved to know that it wasn't forgotten, we leave it for a few more days. The day before the deadline, we've no choice but to face it, and we generally get the item done in half the time we feared it would take!

A list has one big value—recording things before you forget them. As for using a list to discipline yourself, forget it. *You* have to do the things—the list won't do them for you.

A schedule won't do them for you either. I dislike the regimentation of rigid schedules. Set schedules are usually only for inefficient people who are afraid of running out of things to do. Some scheduling and budgeting of time is needed, but not to the extent that it dictates your every move and mood. You should run a schedule for your benefit, not the reverse.

Highs and Lows

The old up-and-down pattern is entrenched in our style of living—but how devastating it is to human feelings and efficient housekeeping! Many of us unthinkingly roll along this way: Once a week (or once a month) we clean the house, water the plants, and do everything just so now we're "up"—ahead of the game. But immediately the spotlessness and satisfaction attained begin to erode as dust, spiders, children, animals, spouse, and guests mount their attack. This is immensely frustrating because we've expended so much dedication and energy getting the house to its peak.

An elderly gentleman recalled his mother's approach to housework: "She organized herself and the family so that all the housework—washing, ironing, baking, sewing, et cetera— was done on Monday (one day, mind you). What an accomplishment! But she spent the other six days recovering to prepare for the big Monday cleanup again."

This kind of cleaning approach gets old fast, and it gets you nowhere except to an early grave. Even if your house is clean as often as it's dirty (meaning it is clean 50 percent of the time), you won't get much credit for it, because it's human nature to notice and respond to the negative, not the positive. Little is heard about the house if it's clean—but if it's dirty, everybody squawks, gossips, and complains. It's demoralizing, but you can't give up the battle. So you buckle down and restore the place to order and cleanliness.

Hold it! Once you've got your house in top shape again, it's time to try something different. A little consistency can save you a lot of time, energy, and discouragement. Avoid the "up-and-down" style of housekeeping. Establish an acceptable cleanliness level and maintain it daily. If you really want to be freed from cleaning drudgery, this one change in style will work wonders for you. When you learn to keep a house on a straight line, you'll not only find extra hours appearing, but some of the other up-and-down styles you've been struggling with for years (exercising, keeping up with the requests at work, cooking, filing, studying, gardening, etc.) will follow your cleaning system and suddenly begin to be manageable. Your home will never stay static. It will be in a constant state of flux if it is actually lived in, as all homes should be. You want to avoid extremes both ways—too much polish is just as disconcerting as too little. Gold-plating a house won't bring you anything but discouragement and worry.

To keep your home in a steady state of cleanliness and livability, you'll learn to wipe down shower walls and plumbing fixtures daily to avoid having to give them an acid bath every month to remove hard-water deposits. You'll carry in a manageable armload of firewood whenever you enter the house, instead of spending a backbreaking hour lugging in a week's worth on Saturday. You'll wipe up spills immediately, when it's five times easier, faster, and much less damaging than putting them off until later.

You'll also discover that **eliminating unnecessary work does wonders for your efficiency,** as does delegating work. If you start delegating, say 60 percent of the daily chores to other household members—you'll be amazed how much the need for picking up the house will decrease.

Do your big yearly cleaning each fall instead of spring; you'll marvel at how much longer the house looks nice. By cleaning *after* the open-window, everyone-in-and-out-all-day season, you keep all that dust, pollen, and dirt from deteriorating your house all winter—with the bonus that the house is cleaner for the winter holidays.

Make a Simple Cleaning Checklist

You may not be able to keep things as spotless as Grandma or Grandpa did—and you may not even want to. With everything else you have going, you may rarely be able to get the cleaning done when you intend to. But, as in everything, it helps to have a map or plan of where you're headed (even if you have to take detours, alternate routes, or shortcuts to get there). An outline of the goal helps you feel calm and in control even when the waves of other agendas and responsibilities are breaking all around you. You don't really want a schedule for cleaning, something that prescribes a precise day and time to do each chore. You want a list or reminder of what needs to be done at approximately what intervals.

Following is a sample of the type of outline professional cleaners use. You may wish to modify or copy it and use it for yourself. Just remember that this is only a very general guide—the number (and age) of the people in your household, your climate, and the type of furnishings and pets you have (if any) will all have a bearing on how often things need to be done.

Daily

- ☐ Straighten up the whole place
- ☐ Do dishes
- ☐ Wipe counters and range top
- ☐ Make beds
- ☐ Dump kitchen garbage
- ☐ Clean up any spots and spills
- ☐ Quick-clean the bathroom (see Chapter 13)
- ☐ Hang up all clothes
- ☐ Read and dispose of mail and magazines
- ☐ Praise any cleaning efforts made by family members

Exterior

- ☐ Police any litter or left-behind tools/toys

Semiweekly

- ☐ Vacuum the most-used areas
- ☐ Sweep or dust-mop hard floors
- ☐ Do laundry

Weekly

- ☐ Vacuum carpets
- ☐ Dust furniture
- ☐ Change beds
- ☐ Spot-clean handprints, etc.

☐ Clean door glass

☐ Clean mirrors

☐ Clean sinks

☐ Clean showers and tubs

☐ Clean the outside of the toilet and use bowl cleaner on the inside

☐ Dump all trash containers

Exterior

☐ Vacuum doormats

☐ Sweep porches

☐ Sweep patios

☐ Haul off any accumulated junk/trash

Monthly

☐ Dust woodwork and high and low areas

☐ Catch all cobwebs

☐ Vacuum upholstery

☐ Vacuum drapes

☐ Dust or vacuum blinds

☐ Sweep or vacuum carpet edges

☐ Rewax heavy traffic areas on waxed floors

☐ Damp-wipe seats of chairs

☐ Clean out refrigerator

☐ Clean kitchen cabinet fronts

☐ Clean appliance fronts and tops

☐ Remove any hard-water buildup

☐ Wash/disinfect trash containers

Exterior

☐ Wash doormats

☐ Sweep or hose walks/driveway

☐ Wash easy-to-reach windows

☐ Spot-clean doors

☐ Sweep garage

Quarterly

☐ Polish furniture

☐ Check and clean or change furnace or central air conditioning filters

☐ Surface-clean carpeting

Twice a Year

☐ Clean oven

☐ Defrost freezer

☐ Degrease stove hood or exhaust fan

☐ Wash vinyl furniture

☐ Turn mattresses

☐ Vacuum air and heat vents

☐ Dust tops of tall furniture, rafters, etc.

☐ Dust/clean light fixtures

Exterior

☐ Check for leaks or pest infestation

Annually

☐ Strip and rewax waxed floors if needed
☐ Wash or dry-sponge walls
☐ Touch up nicks in wall paint
☐ Clean under and behind things
☐ Wash hard-to-reach windows
☐ Wash or dry-clean drapes or curtains
☐ Wash window screens
☐ Clean light fixtures
☐ Wash blinds
☐ Wash/clean blankets
☐ Shampoo carpet/upholstery if needed

Exterior

☐ Clean drain gutters
☐ Wash exterior of all windows
☐ Clean screens/storm doors
☐ Clean siding if needed
☐ Clean/sweep chimney

Every Several Years or So

☐ Wash or otherwise clean ceilings

But remember:
Clean it when it's soiled, not when it's scheduled.

How Much Time Does Housework Actually Take?

We exaggerate three things around the house: "I told you kids a million times," "I haven't slept for two weeks," and "All I do is clean, clean, clean." The last one is an overdone appraisal. We only vacuum seven minutes at a time on the average, spend ten minutes once every ten days cleaning the toilets, wash the walls about once every four years. Many of us dread and dread a task that, if you actually clocked it, takes maybe sixteen minutes. Some of the most procrastinated things (however psychologically formidable) are among the shortest. You can de-cobweb a whole house in a half-hour or less. No matter how it seems, few of us spend "forever" cleaning. We probably average ten hours a week actually housecleaning. The bad aura comes not from cleaning but procrustination— leaving things until they're crusty.

So figure out how long it takes you to do a chore, and see if you can shave off a few minutes each time you do it. This won't just gradually reduce the time you have spent on housework—it'll help you plan better because you'll know how long various jobs actually take. And you'll dread cleaning chores less when you realize they're a matter of minutes, not hours.

Take mood, energy, and motivation into account when you're scheduling and organizing. You're a human being, not a machine. You don't start running at full efficiency the minute you're cranked up. If you try that, you're going to end up mighty discouraged. I can knock out two magazine articles in an hour when I'm fresh, but can't finish one in eight hours when I have the drags. When you're rolling, tackle your most active and demanding work. When the drags invade, file, sort, or do something that requires no creativity or mental energy. In both situations, you're accomplishing a lot by fitting the task to your mood and personality.

Be yourself and decide what's most important to you. Wade into it during your best hours for that particular chore, and a miracle will happen. (You might end up writing a book on organization and selling it back to the supermen and superwomen of the world.)

Chapter Three
Treasure Sorting and Storage Strategy

While helping one of my children move recently, I was vividly reminded of clutter's exponential growth in recent years. Newer, bigger homes are on the rise (no pun intended). Builders cater to our ever-growing desire to acquire things by building in massive amounts of storage space. The larger the house is, the more stuff it has. A teenage girl can have forty-five pairs of shoes—all neatly kept in tote containers with snap-on lids. Boys have box upon box of trading cards, TV- and movie-themed figurines, and Nintendo and PlayStation games and gear (in addition, of course, to all of their old toy cars, trains, and planes). Dad has a deluxe tool inventory and enough golf or fishing tackle to open his own store. Mom has not only a three-closet wardrobe and a couple of file cabinets full of papers, but at least one major hobby requiring a whole constellation of parts, equipment, and supplies. The family's scrapbooking and photo collection doesn't fill just one closet, but a whole room! Decorations used to mean three boxes, stored high in the rafters of the garage. Now there are color-coordinated plastic containers or aged cardboard boxes filled with Easter, Valentine's Day, and the biggie—second only to Christmas in amount—Halloween. Even the pet accessories and equipment can easily fill one of those mini-pickups!

Even young families quickly establish a handsome home filled with elaborate furnishings and decorations, and all kinds of other possessions they spend a large part of their lives collecting, and will spend the rest of their lives cleaning and keeping track of.

Most of us are in the same condition. Our treasures may not be expensive, but we have as many of them crammed in as many cubbyholes—which we shuffle through, sort and re-sort, climb over, worry about, and maintain for hours on end. What does any of it contribute to our lives or personal edification? Even the Salvation Army store would label most of it "junk." Junk has frustrated more people than toys that evade assembly at midnight on Christmas Eve. It's burned down more homes, caused more indigestion, and resulted in more arguments than can be imagined. And for what reason: Accumulation? Sentiment? Security? Who knows?

Some percentage of the "stuff" that we have stored or lying around somewhere may be of some worth to us. But this is often about 30 percent of what we own. Why have a houseful of useless objects that rob you of time and energy?

Kicking the Junk Habit

It's amazing how we get ourselves into the junk habit. **As the Law of the Pack Rat goes, "Junk will accumulate in proportion to the storage room available for it."** Before learning the shortcuts and professional methods of cleaning a house, we must first learn the art of "treasure sorting." This means differentiating between valuable and useless things and promptly disposing of the latter. You can't palm off this job on anyone else, or postpone it too long, because there's no escape from the toll that junk takes on your life. It might be out of the middle of the room, but it's not out of mind. No matter how deep something is buried in a cupboard or storage compartment, it's there and it weighs on you. Once you get rid of a piece of junk, it's discarded from your mind and you're free from keeping mental tabs on it.

For example, people maintain second homes mentally and physically for the entire year, yet often only use them for a couple of weeks. If it were possible to calculate the emotional energy that's silently burned up worrying about the second home, it would surely outweigh the benefits of a couple of weeks or months occupying it.

We are also burdened by the feeling of obligation to use our junk—whether we need it or not. If we don't or can't use it, then we worry about why we have it at all! Junk will get you—don't sit there and argue that it won't.

The most valuable "someday useful" junk will stymie your emotional freedom if not handled properly. Inasmuch as all of us feel guilty and frustrated about our piles of junk, we have to eliminate the problem. In turn, it will eliminate an unbelievable amount of housework.

How Junk Begins

There's a reason we quit using something. It's outdated, broken, unsafe, unattractive, or inoperable, which means, we don't need it anymore—except, of course, for sentimental value. As each day goes by, it becomes more outdated, less safe, more unattractive, and will remain broken and inoperable. So learn to follow the 70/30 law that a magazine publisher made famous. He held up an ordinary magazine and said, "Look, 70 percent of this magazine is advertising." So anyone who has any magazines or newspapers lying in boxes or piles around the house has up to 70 percent junk (depending on how healthy ad sales are). The first time you go through a magazine, remove any article of interest to you and throw the junk away. If you start doing this regularly, you'll rejoice for having eliminated those hernia-causing, guilt-producing boxes of magazines. Instead of piles of magazines, you'll have a thin, usable file of articles you want.

Other junk can be treated the same way. The faucet leaks and the handles are corroded, so we replace them with a sleek new chrome beauty. But we can't bear to throw the old ones away, because some day (even though they're broken, outdated, unattractive, and inoperable) we just might need a washer out of them. So we put them in the junk drawer or closet or hang them in the garage to get tangled up in the bicycle spokes. We could have removed the washers in two minutes and thrown the rest in the garbage, saving hours over a lifetime of shuffling the old faucet around and dodging it. What a mighty grip junk has on us! We'll keep that worthless worn-out faucet for fifteen years, then in our move to Denver or Boston, into a new house, guess what we take with us . . . yes, the old faucet. We never know when we might need it. The average American moves eleven times in a lifetime. If a third of your stuff is clutter, imagine how much space and money you could save if you dejunked! People spend literally millions moving junk.

No matter how we may rationalize—"Oh well, we can put it in the attic," or "There's room in the basement"—that junk should go to the dump, to the recycler, or in the Goodwill bag. The number one secret of staying junk-free is to make the decision *at the time that something is to be put away.* Because once you store it, sentimental attachment and mental obligation to use it (to justify the storage) begin to mount. And we never take the time later to go back through all that stored stuff and decide.

Another good way to come to terms with junk is to face the fact of just how much room is truly available for storage. If you can't conveniently store an item, then you can't use it conveniently.

The Costs of Clutter

Keeping something anywhere will cost you: a little bit of space and rent, a little bit of energy (heat and lights), a little bit of accident and fire potential, a little bit of insurance and moth- and burglar-proofing money, a little bit of your emotions, a little bit of respect (from those who laugh at you behind your back for saving dumb things, even if they do it, too). All of these little costs of keeping stuff add up to a big price tag.

Stored junk and clutter is also prime fuel for arguments. Fights, resentments, grudges, and even divorces can come from stored stuff. Every day, a little money and a little merit slips away as that stored stuff rots and goes out of style. When a piece of my neighbor's farm machinery wore out and became worthless, he would pull it out onto the field to save it for "parts." Year after year, as the older implements rusted, fresh clutter was lined up, until he covered five acres of good farm ground. The total "parts" saved might have been worth $600 at most, while the total value for the crops lost due to inactive acreage was closer to $11,000. Great economy, eh?

A woman bought and stored 900 yards of fabric to sew up "someday"—she wanted to have it just in case. When she was in her nineties, she still had 876 yards of polyester stockpiled for . . . someday.

It's the "maybes" that get you

My company cleans lots of homes after floods and fires ("restoration" work for insurance companies). I have seen many sad sights in the course of it—all of that stored stuff, usually charred or soaking in sewer water, has to be pawed through while every relative and friend helping gasps and expresses wonderment as to why anyone would keep all this. Talk about heartbreaks and wallet aches—storage will do it every time. One insurance man who handles losses in those self-storage complexes said that when they're robbed or when there is a fire, most of the owners can't remember half of what was in there (all that stuff they were so carefully keeping and paying room and board for). Often the storage cost of an article is far higher than the cost of replacing it; it's not uncommon for people to pay $400 a year to rent a storage spot for $200 worth of stuff.

But these things are valuable, you say? What about the value of life and time to store, to clean, to insure, to transport, to protect—what does that cost? "Afford" is not simply a question of money. What is the effect on your job, your physical being, your peace of mind? "Afford" is the capacity to absorb into your being—not into your bank balance.

Think about the storage problem in your home. A lot of that stuff you're storing is useless. It's a constant source of worry. Most of it is unsafe, outdated, and ugly, so why keep it? Why spend a valuable part of yourself polishing, washing, dusting, and thinking about it?

You can't afford junk. It will rob you physically, emotionally, and spiritually. Freeing yourself from junk will automatically free you from much of your housework (and it won't take any soap and water either). A cluttered house takes *much* more time and effort to clean. You double your cleaning time by having to "pick up" a cluttered house, but even a neat house will take longer to clean than it should if there's too much furniture or it's overdecorated.

Clutter is one of the greatest enemies of efficiency and stealers of time. For every chore tackled, we usually spend more time getting ready—hunting for a place, tools, and supplies to do it—than actually doing it. It takes only six seconds to drive a nail, but ten minutes to find the nails and hammer. Junk makes every job harder and makes cleaning take forever. Any project we tackle, from building to disassembling, will be slowed, dampened, and diluted if we constantly have to fight our way to it in the midst of clutter.

If junk is taking up your storage space, you have to reach farther and dig deeper to get the tool, book, suitcase, shirt, or whatever you need. "Getting something out," instead of being a few-seconds job, often ends up a twenty-minute search-and-rescue mission.

*When I say "dejunk," I don't mean sort your four
cubbyholes of worthless stuff into three cubbyholes
of worthless stuff—or I'll tell on you!*

Now, don't say, "Oh, I know my junk has got to go, and one of these days, I'm going to . . . " There are more reasons than ease of cleaning to dejunk your house (and your life). This might surprise you, but it's a reality: Many people are buried so deep in junk that no one can navigate through all the clutter to get to them. Your mate or son or daughter can't give you attention and affection until he or she can find you. I've cleaned (or tried to clean) hundreds of homes where lonely, frustrated men and women, buried in junk, can't understand why they and their families aren't closer. Junk is the barrier! Junk (and junk projects and activities) prevents you from being available for affection or opportunity. Too often the things we save and store end up as tombstones for us. Boxes of mummified prom corsages and piles of corroded hubcaps will bury you.

If having piles, rooms, or buildings full of junk (even if it is labeled "antique") is worth all those hours to shuffle it and all that mental energy to keep track of it, then you may value junk more than your time and freedom. If having a closet full of gleaming silver is worth hours of polishing time a month, you may enjoy impressing people more than you value your time and freedom. Nothing exists in and of itself. Everything has a cost to acquire and to maintain. The majority of the cost you pay with your time and energy.

Eliminate the junk around your house. It's one of the easiest ways to free yourself from household imprisonment. If you think you need emotional permission and physical direction to dejunk, check out my books on the subject, including *Clutter's Last Stand, 2nd Edition,* and *Weekend Makeover.*

Chapter Four

What to Expect from the Rest of the Family

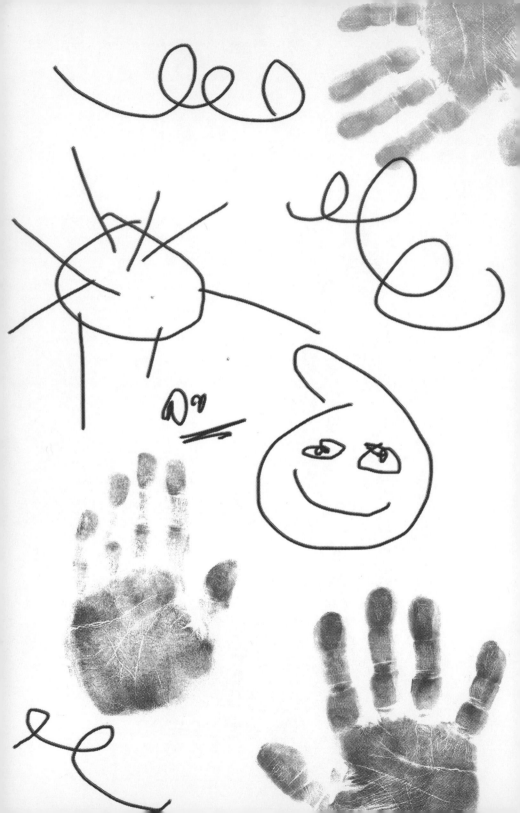

Well, this might be what you get by way of help from some family members, but it is for sure not what you should expect. Actually, the woman of the house—already responsible for the majority of home and family related matters—should expect the rest of the household (including guests and freeloaders) to do most of the housework. If all of the areas and items needing to be cleaned and cared for in a house were actually assigned to those who created the need for cleaning or repair, the average woman would have very little to do in the upkeep department. My apologies, in advance, to those lucky enough to have families that do their fair share around the house.

The lack of help and cooperation from many men and children is a grim reality still, but it doesn't have to be.

It's not circumstance that causes you to have a messy house and spend two hours cleaning when you could spend fifteen minutes. It's you—and your own willingness to accept or not accept things. You don't need to engage in open rebellion or use brute force, but you can try the following:

1. *Refuse to be the janitor for the family messes.* Picking up after them is bad for everyone involved. You teach irresponsibility when you assume someone else's responsibility (except those who don't know any better or can't help themselves). Insist that everyone clean up his or her own messes and premises. Once they're out of diapers, if they're old enough to mess up, they're old enough to clean up!

2. *Write down and post needs.* When you ask for help, most family members will assist you. Written lists eliminate short memories and the innocent phrase, "I didn't know you needed anything done."

3. *Make it easy for them to help.* To encourage bed making, for instance, use one heavy blanket instead of several thinner ones (better yet, invest in attractive comforters that can serve as a blanket and bedspread). Teach the kids to spread the sheet and blanket and then circle the bed once, tucking as they go. Make sure everyone has plenty of bins and hangers for personal belongings, and the house will be tidier. If you need a visual aid to teach the family to clean, get a copy of my video "Is There Life After Housework?" In ninety fast-paced and fun minutes, they'll learn everything they need to know.

4. *Be patient and be persistent.* Things don't change just because you say they will. You have to stick with it. The biggest threat to success here is the "If you can't beat 'em, join 'em" syndrome. Hang in there. Refuse to pick up the slack for nonperformers. Don't fall back on "It's easier to do it myself than to get them to do it." If you work to make others clean up after themselves, you'll eventually get them trained and you won't have to worry about it. But if you break down and do it yourself, you'll be doing it for the rest of your life. Just remember—it's as much for their good as it is for yours. So stand your ground!

5. *Use praise lavishly when it's deserved.* Appeal to their vanity (this may work especially well on men). Remember, you can catch more flies with honey than vinegar.

The two blank pages at the beginning of this chapter (which my audiences have chuckled at for years) have now expanded to a whole book, *HELP! Around the House: A Mother's Guide to Getting the Family to Pitch In and Clean Up,* to help you accomplish the mission of getting the whole family to help out.

Chapter Five

The Old Wives' Tales...
Ever Hear These?

"Never shampoo carpets when they're new; they get dirty faster."
"Use newspaper to polish your windows."
"Toothpaste and peanut butter remove black marks."
"Spring is the best time to clean!"
"Start washing from the bottom of the wall and work up."
"Dried bread crumbs clean wallpaper."

Even if some of these might possibly work—why go the long way around to get the job done? Carpets don't get dirty faster after the first shampooing if you do it right. Newspapers aren't good for polishing (only for training puppies and peeking at the comics). Toothpaste and peanut butter do remove marks because they're abrasive—but they also cut the gloss of good enamel paint, and the resulting dull patch looks worse than the original mark. Spring isn't the best time to clean indoors—late fall is. Who wants to be cooped up with paint and ammonia fumes when springtime blossoms are fragrant? If you wash a wall from the bottom, when you get to the top dirty water will run down onto the freshly cleaned bottom.

For centuries, "secrets" of cleaning homebrews have been passed down from mothers and grandmothers. These ineffective formulas are whispered down to the next generation so that even in this day of modern science, well-educated home cleaners living in up-to-the-minute homes are still following outdated remedies—using powdered moth whiskers to remove grease stains, crumbled cottage cheese to polish brass doorknobs and dried bread crumbs to clean wallpaper. I have yet to find a magic cleaner that will take all the work out of cleaning a house. Less than 10 percent of the hundreds of old wives' tales sent or repeated to me ever *worked*. And there's no magic in the bottle, either. Even if the latest cleaning miracle on TV is as good as advertisers say it is, it will have little effect on your cleaning time.

It's not what you clean with so much as how you go about it that really matters. So forget the old wives' tales you've heard and commercials you've seen, and follow some simple professional methods that have been used efficiently and safely for decades.

Whatever you do, don't feel it's your patriotic or economic duty to mix up your own money-saving brew. Some of the results are ridiculous. Home cleaners trying to make their own furniture polish can spend three hours rounding up the materials and mixing up a solution that costs $7.50 for ingredients alone, instead of buying a commercial polish for $2.49 that's tested, safe, and guaranteed not to ferment, explode, or ruin the furniture. Remember, today more than ever, it's your time that's valuable. In the professional cleaning industry or at home, the cost of materials and supplies is a very small part of the equation. A half-century of professional cleaner's records show that for every dollar spent for cleaning, only five or six cents is for supplies and equipment; almost the same ratio holds true in the home. Your time and safety are the valuable commodities, not the supplies.

Most home brews are misguided formulations. For instance, most homemade furniture polishes call for linseed oil—a penetrant that conditions raw wood. When smeared on *finished* wood (which most furniture is), however, it forms a sticky film that acts as a magnet to every passing speck of dust. Many home cleaners pour chlorine bleach into everything from mop water to toilet bowls, to no avail—bleach is an oxidizing agent that doesn't clean a thing. And don't spend your precious hours grinding and rubbing trying to get vinegar to perform like soap. Vinegar isn't a cleaner, it's a rinsing agent. The "squeak" is what turns you on!

Looking at this from a "free me from housework" angle, using good, efficient—even expensive—supplies and equipment is a cheap way to go if it cuts your time down. For example, if you pay $22 for a gallon of floor finish, it's a wise buy if it means that whatever you apply it to will only need annual or biennial cleaning and waxing.

Your Household Tools Are Your Power Tools

Cleaning equipment is often overlooked in our spending priorities. Over and over, I see old rattletrap vacuums hardly capable of running, let alone sucking up any dirt. The hose is full of holes, and the cord is worn and offers instant electrocution if touched in the wrong place. Every day we wrestle these machines to do the housework, while in the family room sits $2,500 worth of computer equipment, in the basement and garage sit $400 radial-arm saws

and other power tools that haven't been used in six months, or thousands of dollars worth of boats or snow machines that may be used a few days a year. The kitchen junk drawer (you know, that drawer with all the parts, spare tools, lids, screws, handles, matches, nails, etc.) is used more by the average family than an $800 solid oak workbench. Time is our most valuable commodity, and good housecleaning tools and equipment can save hundreds of hours a year.

Take a good look around your home, and consider your cleaning routines. The tools likely to be used most and those capable of saving the most time are the ones to upgrade or buy. Anything that can be purchased to save time in housework is just as important as a new computer is for business! (And don't spend all the money on little-used and often useless "trinket" attachments to cleaning machines or appliances. Concentrate on solid, basic tools and supplies.)

What's a Home Cleaner to Do?

Forget the witch potions and the glamorously packaged, overpriced household cleaners you've been using. Almost every telephone business directory in the country lists janitorial-supply stores. These are wholesale outlets where professional cleaning companies buy many of their supplies. Professionals buy the rest at a local supermarket, same as you do. In a janitorial-supply store, you'll find the items that can't be bought at the supermarket, discount, or hardware store. The prices at janitorial-supply stores vary, but I've never run into one that wouldn't sell to anyone who stepped in the door.

You can buy professional cleaning products wholesale or retail and the price of either is better than the price of comparable supplies at the supermarket. The best way to try for a wholesale price is to walk in with dignity and authority, squinting confidently at the shelves of cleaning material and equipment (few of which you'll recognize the first time), and say, "I'm Mrs. Van Snoot of Snoot, Frisky, and Melvin [you, your cat, and your dog—the more you sound like a law firm, the better]. I need one gallon of metal interlock self-polishing floor finish." This usually convinces the seller that you're official, and he or she will generally offer you the contractor's price, since most suppliers are great people and run "hungry" establishments. If the supplier asks you a question like, "Do you want polymer or carnauba base?" don't lose your nerve. Just say, "Give me the house's bestselling brand." If you don't get the contractor's price, you'll at least get a discount.

Which Supplies to Use Where and When?

As we cover each area of cleaning, we'll go over the supplies you should use. Just remember: There's no magic in the bottle or machine. The basics of effective cleaning are extremely simple, and you need just a few professional supplies. A chart at the end of this chapter lists the basic tools you'll find useful. A home will be well prepared for efficient cleaning and maintenance if it's equipped with the items listed. (If you can't find them, write me at the address on page 49 and I'll send you a mail-order catalog.)

"Miracle" solutions and "magic" tools aren't the only carryover from old wives' tales. Newspaper and magazine household advice columns are everywhere. "Helpful hints" often only add frustration. Be discerning, and check sources when you choose housecleaning advice.

You can do without advice like "Drop a couple of rose petals in your vacuum bag so you can deodorize as you clean," or "Color-coordinate all your bathrooms so the towels will match and you'll always be ready for unexpected company."

What you need to learn most of all is how to choose and use supplies and materials so as to use fewer hours of your time to have a cleaner home than you've ever had before. Life after housework is life left over for happiness—for family, for friends, for self—and you're entitled to that.

By the way—did you know that a paste of strawberries, wheat germ, ground glass, and baking soda will polish the bottom of a camper's cooking kit? (But so will a 17 cent scouring pad!)

Proper Supplies = Big Returns

There are more benefits in using the right equipment and supplies than merely doing a faster and better job. They are:

- **Safety**—You'll be using fewer, simpler items that will be safer to use and easier to store out of children's reach.
- **Reduced cost**—In the long run you'll spend a lot less on cleaning supplies if you select and use them properly.
- **Lessened depreciation**—Using the proper cleaning supplies and tools reduces damage to and deterioration of the surfaces and structures you're cleaning.
- **Savings on storage space**—Fewer and more efficient supplies (including concentrates) take up less of the storage space you probably don't have enough of anyway.

If your cleaning closet is full of cans, bottles, and boxes, I promise a roomier closet once you learn the secrets of proper cleaning. Many of those chemicals and cleaners crammed into every cupboard and under every sink aren't all that effective. They use up valuable room, they're safety hazards for children, and many of them actually damage household surfaces.

Most people's cleaning-supply storage areas (under the sink, in the pantry, or in the closet) look like Thomas Edison's chemical cache—just seconds before the explosion. Many of these things simply get wasted because we forget to use them.

Cleaning Up with Concentrates

Concentrates are much cheaper than ordinary household cleaning products. They take a lot less room to store, and because they're professional products (hair spray, deodorizers, medicines, lubricants, paints, even food), they do a better job.

The aerosol can has pressured itself into the lives of all. Many products come in aerosol because we've been convinced that the easiest approach is to just push a button. We've carried this principle over into our housecleaning systems, paying dollars for pennies' worth of cleaners and compressed gas. Yes, aerosols are convenient, and some of them may use a propellant that doesn't harm the environment. But considering the small amount of cleaner you get this way, how easily the nozzle clogs, and the dangerous can you have to dispose of afterward, **it's cheaper and more environmentally sound to dilute your own concentrated cleaners into professional plastic spray bottles.** They last and last, you can see what's in them at any time, and you can control the spray to be a mist or a stream. Some insecticide, paint, and grooming products are hard to beat in aerosol, but when it comes to cleaning, go with the spray bottles for speed, economy, and safety.

To replace most of the aerosols and supermarket pump-spray products you now use, go to the janitorial-supply store and buy four or five reusable professional plastic spray bottles. Buy your chemicals, cleaners, and disinfectants by the concentrated gallon. Cleaning concentrates are also available in little plastic packets (like those little single servings of ketchup or mustard), preventing waste and wrong dilution, and making storage and handling a cinch. They're premeasured for use in a bucket or spray bottle—just snip them open and mix with water as directed on the label. Being able to bring a year's worth of cleaning supplies home in a small sack and store them safely in a little lockable drawer instead of under the sink is the thing of the future. And using concentrates reduces the number of aerosols we use and the number of empty containers to be disposed of.

Mixing and Using Concentrates

Mix concentrates with water at the suggested dilution ratios and put the solutions in the spray bottles. When mixing up cleaners from concentrate, fill the bottle with water before you add the concentrate. You won't have 4 inches of foam in the bottle this way, and it prevents chemical splashes, too. Label each bottle with a waterproof marker or make sure each chemical is a different color, lest you end up cleaning the windows with upholstery shampoo. These plastic spray bottles are sturdy and durable, won't nick cupboards, and are extremely efficient and economical to use—whether for heavy-duty cleaning or smaller "keep-up" jobs.

Be sure to properly dilute cleaners. Our tendency is to say, "If a little does a good job, a lot will do better." This is as silly as saying, "If a teaspoon of baking powder will make the biscuits rise, then a cup should do wonders." We often *gluggy-glug-glug* too much soap into the water and actually destroy the chemical's dirt-suspending and grease-cutting action. Read the directions! Remember, you don't clean alone. You have two helpers, water and chemicals; they'll do most of the work.

The cleaning compounds described in this chart and elsewhere in this book are no more dangerous than many preparations found on supermarket shelves. But since most janitorial supplies do not come with childproof lids, be sure to keep them out of the reach of children.

Neutral Cleaner—the Home Cleaner's Best Friend

Neutral cleaner is a cleaner that's mild and safe enough for most any surface because it's neither acid nor alkaline.

You Need Only Four Basic Cleaners

1. **Neutral all-purpose cleaner:** Neither alkaline nor acidic, so it can be used for almost any type of cleaning and is safe for most surfaces

2. **Disinfectant cleaner:** For bathrooms and other areas needing germicidal action (Buy only a quaternary type—it's relatively nontoxic and won't damage most surfaces.)

3. **Heavy-duty cleaner/degreaser:** A high-pH cleaner with good emulsifying action for tough cleaning jobs where grease is a problem

4. **Glass cleaner:** Usually alcohol or ammonia based, so it evaporates quickly without leaving streaks or residue (For cleaning small windows, polishing mirrors, appliances, tiles, etc.)

A detergent doesn't have to be strictly neutral (have a pH of 7) to qualify—it just has to be somewhere close to neutral. Most neutral cleaners have a pH in the range of 7 to 9. Professionals use these cleaners for many light-duty cleaning jobs, such as floor mopping and wall washing, that call for streak-free results with no detergent residue. Arm yourself with a big supply of neutral cleaner to handle the majority of the cleaning chores around the house safely and inexpensively by going to a janitorial-supply store and getting a jug of "neutral all-purpose cleaner concentrate." (It's even available with a pump-dispenser top.) Then just dilute with water as needed and use.

Professional Equipment and Supplies

For your convenience, those items marked * are available by mail. For more information and a free catalog, write to: The Clean Report, PO Box 700, Pocatello, ID 83204, or visit Don Aslett's Cleaning Center online at *www.cleanreport.com*.

Must-Have Equipment and Supplies

Item	Size/Type	Use	Source
Microfiber cloth*	Various sizes	This revolutionary material cleans and sanitizes without any chemicals. Use with plain water on nearly any surface—glass to carpet, stovetops to dashboards. Use dry for polishing and lint-free dusting. Machine washable and reuseable.	Widely available
Cleaning cloth*	Made from 18" × 18" piece of cotton terrycloth; replaces the "rag"	Can be used for most cleaning jobs; especially effective in wall and ceiling cleaning. The tube style cloth can be folded and refolded to provide 16 cleaning surfaces. (See Chapter 15 for details on how to make and use a cleaning cloth.)	Homemade; also available from the Cleaning Center
Masslinn cloth*	11 " × 17 " disposable	For dusting. The specially treated paper "cloth" collects dust instead of scattering it. Leaves soft sheen on furniture without creating buildup. Perfect for computer screens and all electronics, handy to keep in the car.	Janitorial-supply stores
Cellulose sponge*	Various sizes; choose one that fits your hand comfortably	For any washing or absorbing job. Always squeeze, never wring.	Widely available
Window squeegee*	Brass or stainless steel frame, rubber blade; 10" or 12" blade for average size panes; 16" or 18" blade for very large panes (Ettore is a good brand.)	Strictly for window cleaning. Avoid contact with rough surfaces so rubber blade will stay perfectly smooth. Use with extension handle for high windows (see Optional Professional Equipment Chart).	Janitorial-supply stores

Must-Have Equipment and Supplies

Item	Size/Type	Use	Source
Lambswool duster*	Large puff of lambswool on a handle; many sizes, including long and short handles and duster heads that fit on extension handles	Picks up dust by static attraction. Useful for high dusting, ceiling fans, picture frames, moldings, ledges, blinds, books, cobwebs, houseplants, etc.	Janitorial-supply stores and others
Scrub sponge*	White nylon-backed scrub sponge	Use where gentle abrasion is needed; always wet before using. The white nylon side will not harm household surfaces. Good in the bathroom and kitchen. (Dark-colored pads like the harsher green nylon variety can scratch and damage household surfaces.)	Widely available
Spray bottle*	Quart or 22-ounce plastic bottle with professional-quality trigger sprayer	To use with cleaning solutions you mix up yourself from cleaner concentrate and water. For general cleaning, bathrooms, small windows, or spot cleaning. Keep several around the house in convenient locations.	Janitorial-supply stores
Dry sponge* (One of my favorite cleaning tools.)	5" × 7" × ½" pad of natural open-cell rubber	"Dry cleans" whatever it is rubbed across. Use on acoustical tile, flat-painted walls, wallpaper, lampshades, oil paintings, fireplaces, and to remove pet hair from furniture. Cleans many surfaces better, faster, and less messily than liquid cleaners. Discard when dirt-saturated.	Paint stores or janitorial-supply stores

Must-Have Equipment and Supplies

Item	Size/Type	Use	Source
Dust mop*	14" or 18" cotton head, swivel handle	The fast and efficient way to "sweep" hard floors. Use with dust treatment for best results. Shake out and vacuum head regularly; launder when dirt-saturated, then re-treat.	Janitorial-supply stores and others
Sponge mop	10" or 12" professional-quality sponge mop with no-stoop, easy-pull wringer and changeable head	For damp-mopping small amounts of hard flooring.	Janitorial-supply stores
Long-handled floor scrubber* (also called a Scrubbee Doo or Doodlebug)	Long-handled tool to which a variety of heads can be attached.	For effortless scrubbing of hard floors, showers, baseboards, concrete—almost anything. (I wouldn't trade mine for a gold-plated floor machine.) The holder comes prepacked with nylon pads of three different strengths for light, medium, and heavy-duty scrubbing. Dust mop, microfiber, mopping, and wax applicator heads are also available.	Besides the Cleaning Center, also available at some stores that sell cleaning gear, such as department stores
Floor squeegee*	18" or 24" push-pull (Ettore is the brand I use.)	For floor cleaning, picking up water, and drying sidewalks and garage floors. Use instead of slop mop when stripping or refinishing a hard floor. (See Chapter 10 for detailed instructions on using a floor squeegee when stripping a floor.)	Janitorial-supply stores
Bowl swab*	Cotton or rayon head on a plastic handle	Enables you to use bowl cleaner neatly and safely. Use to force water out of the toilet bowl and swab around interior of bowl (see p. 192).	Janitorial-supply stores

Must-Have Equipment and Supplies

Item	Size/Type	Use	Source
Mats (indoor and outdoor)*	3' × 4', 3' × 5', or 3' × 6'; nylon, olefin, or polypropylene fiber on vinyl or rubber backing for inside or covered exteriors; AstroTurf mats for outside	Absorb mud and water from foot traffic and help keep dust, grit, and other debris from being tracked in.	Janitorial-supply stores and others; mail order
Upright vacuum*	Commercial model with beater brush and onboard tools; choose one with 12" or wider head and a long cord	For carpet and rugs, plus above-floor vacuuming.	Janitorial-supply or vacuum stores
Wet-dry vacuum	10-gallon metal or plastic tank, with squeegee, upholstery, and edge tool attachments (Be sure to get one with a a rust-resistant tank and squeegee, upholstery, and edge tool attachments.)	Can be used like a canister vacuum for all household vacuuming, as well as to pick up water when scrubbing floors, or to pick up spills and overflows.	Widely available
Neutral all-purpose cleaner*	Concentrate—packet, quart, or gallon size	Dilute as directed for mopping, spray-cleaning, cleaning painted surfaces, and all general cleaning where a disinfectant isn't needed. Mild, gentle cleaner that won't damage household surfaces. Streak-free formula recommended, such as Clean & Brite.	Janitorial-supply stores

Must-Have Equipment and Supplies

Item	Size/Type	Use	Source
Disinfectant cleaner*	Quaternary type, concentrate—gallon or packet size	Dilute as directed for use in bathroom cleaning and wherever else sanitation is essential. More effective than bleach on mold.	Janitorial-supply stores
Fast-evaporating glass cleaner*	Concentrate—packet, quart, or gallon size	Dilute as directed to clean small windows, mirrors, appliances, chrome, etc.	Janitorial-supply stores
Heavy-duty cleaner/degreaser*	Concentrate—packet, quart, or gallon size	For tough cleaning jobs, especially where grease is a problem (vent fans, top of refrigerator, kitchen walls, etc.).	Janitorial-supply stores
Professional wax remover*	Non-ammoniated—quart or gallon size	For removing wax and floor finish from hard-surface floors.	Janitorial-supply stores
Floor finish ("wax")*	Quart or gallon size, acrylic or metal interlock self-polishing	To protect hard floor surfaces—vinyl, no-wax, linoleum, sealed concrete, sealed wood, and more.	Janitorial-supply stores
Oil soap*	A mild soap often made of vegetable oil	Cleans wood safely and leaves a soft sheen on wood furniture, paneling, etc.	Widely available

Must-Have Equipment and Supplies

Item	Size/Type	Use	Source
Spotter, water-based	Quart or gallon	Use to remove stains from fabric, carpet, and upholstery. Keep in a handy location to grab quickly when spills happen.	Widely available
Spotter, solvent	Quart or gallon	For oily and waxy stains, tar; also removes labels and gummy residue. (De-Solv-It is the brand I use.) Follow label directions; do not use on carpet without pretesting on a remnant.	Widely available
Bacteria/ enzyme digester	Quart or gallon	Live, friendly bacteria eat organic matter to remove nasty odors and stains: urine, feces, vomit.	Janitorial-supply stores

Optional Professional Equipment

Item	Size/Type	Use	Source
Extension handle*	Extends from 4' to 8', 10', or 18'; aluminum or fiberglass, rubber handle	Lightweight, easy to use—the safe way to reach high places. Fits squeegees, window-washing wands, paint rollers, dusters, etc.	Janitorial-supply stores
Window scrubber*	10" or 18" fleece head	Use to apply cleaning solution to window prior to squeegeeing. Great for high windows. Fits extension handle.	Janitorial-supply stores
Wet mop*	12, 16, or 24 oz. rayon/cotton; screw-type handle for easy head replacement (Layflat is a good brand.)	For damp-mopping if you have a great deal of hard flooring.	Janitorial-supply stores

Optional Professional Equipment

Item	Size/Type	Use	Source
Mop bucket*	18-quart metal or plastic with self-contained roller wringer	If you wet-mop, the self-contained wringer saves injuries from hand wringing. Use for mopping—or as a punchbowl at a janitor's wedding.	Janitorial-supply stores
Pumice stone*	Small bar or block of pumice	To remove accumulated hard-water ring in toilet. (Not for use on tubs, bold-colored fixtures, or tile.) Always wet before using.	Janitorial-supply stores
Shower cleaner*	Professional-strength; quart or gallon	A combination of acids and grease cutter such as Showers-n-Stuff that works anywhere in the bathroom that hard-water deposits, soap scum, and body oils accumulate.	Janitorial-supply stores
Professional all-purpose scrub brush (often called "utility brush")*	Nylon bristles and handle; various sizes	For scrubbing without getting your hand wet or scraped.	Janitorial-supply stores
Cleaning caddy*	Plastic (pick a bright color so it's easy to keep track of)	The easy way to carry all your supplies with you as you clean room to room. Keep one conveniently under every sink, filled with everything you need.	Widely available
Angle broom*	Professional-quality plastic broom, with split-tip nylon bristles	For quick cleanups, sweeping small areas, and doing edges and corners before vacuuming or dust-mopping.	Janitorial-supply stores

Optional Professional Equipment

Item	Size/Type	Use	Source
Push broom*	Professional-quality with 18" or 24" head, nylon bristles, handle brace	For sweeping sidewalks, driveways, and unsealed concrete.	Janitorial-supply stores
Pet rake*	12" crimped nylon bristles	For removing pet hair from furniture, bedding, carpets, and clothing.	Available only through the Cleaning Center

Green Clean

In the old days, "bright" and "shiny" was what we were all after. Now, with ozone depletion, pollution, litter, algae overgrowth, toxic waste, and too much solid waste of all kinds to worry about, keeping things "green" is the battle cry of concerned cleaners. None of us wants to ruin our home planet while cleaning, so strong solvents, acids, and other dangerous chemicals and abrasive cleaning materials are getting pretty unpopular in the social circle of the clean. I agree that the real clean is green, and here are some simple, practical things you can do to help out:

1. *Buy good, solid cleaning gear and take care of it.* Brooms, squeegees, vacuums, etc., can last twenty-plus years. That means less energy and fewer raw materials used in manufacturing, and less worn-out tools being disposed of.

2. *Simplify.* As explained in this chapter, you don't need fifty different cleaning preparations or scores of cleaning machines and attachments.

3. *Use concentrates.* If you get premeasured cleaner concentrates (see page 47), you can bring a year's worth of supplies home in a small sack. Fewer bottles and containers will be left to litter and to bury. Not transporting all that

water contained in ready-to-use cleaners also saves on shipping and energy costs.

4. *Do it right.* Skillful cleaning cuts 75 percent or more of the time you spend cleaning, and that means three-quarters of all the lights, heat, water, gas, and other energy consumed in cleaning is cut as well. And it prevents premature wear and destruction of paint, carpet, hard flooring, and other household furnishings and surfaces.

5. *Use no more than you need.* And use the gentlest cleaner that will do the job.

6. *Take advantage of preventive measures.* Use mats, maintenance-free design, sealing, etc. This will cut down the need to redo or to clean at all, saving energy, supplies, packaging, etc.

If we all took just these six steps every day, starting tomorrow, it would help a lot. Remember, you don't have to wait until everyone else does it. Be a leader: Think green when you clean.

Chapter Six

Relax, and Work Less

A big event was coming to a small town and in preparation, the townspeople resolved to clean the floor in the village recreation center. They decided to scrub all the dirt and old wax buildup from the floor and apply a new coat of finish. The committee in charge chose six of the best housecleaners and the building's janitor to do the job. It took the group of seven most of a Saturday to finish it. For six hours the group labored, spending a total of forty-two man-hours to get the floor ready for the finish application.

Several years later, after much hard use, the floor again needed attention. I had a free day, and since I enjoy cleaning floors, I volunteered to do the job at no charge. I refused the help of other volunteers and the janitor, and instead used my sons, who were twelve and eight years old. We showed up at 10:30 in the morning and went home early for lunch at 11:45. The job was completed perfectly in just over an hour, or for the three of us, a total of less than four man-hours in all, much less than the forty-two hours used by the group. We used three fewer mops, half the cleaners and strippers, and one-tenth the hot water—and did a much better job. I'm not any faster a worker than most of you, nor did I have any secret tools. Any of you could have done the same thing using a valuable principle of cleaning: Relax, and work less. To relate this principle more directly to the domestic front, let's take a glimpse of a young home cleaner in action.

It's been an unbelievable morning for Karen. In addition to her own five children, fourteen friends and relatives, caught in a snowstorm, were overnight guests in her home. They consumed dozens of whole-wheat pancakes, eggs, and other breakfast goodies. Two hours later, our heroine finally saw her unexpected guests depart and the children off to school.

She then turned to restoring the kitchen to livable condition. The splatters of batter, jam, and grease covering her stove and countertop were now hard and dry. She began scrubbing one end of the counter furiously. Finally loosening or wearing away the drops of batter in one spot, she'd move on another few inches to grind some more of the droplets away. Twenty minutes of exhausting effort later, the range and counter were presentable.

The Universal Law of Cleaning

Karen could have saved more than fifteen minutes and been easier on the kitchen surfaces if she had used the cleaning principle my sons and I used on the floor. You could call it the universal law of cleaning: Eliminate, saturate, dissolve, remove. You can do 75 percent of your cleaning with your head, not your hands, because 75 percent of soil removal is done chemically, not by elbow grease. Scrubbing to clean something went out with beating your clothes on a rock by the riverside.

Karen needs only to sweep all the loose food particles from the countertop (*eliminate*: fifteen seconds). She should then soak a dishcloth in soapy water and generously wet the entire area (*saturate*: fifteen seconds), giving the liquid a few minutes to soak and loosen the spatters. Then, she merely has to wipe the mushy residue off *(remove)*. Just five minutes or less for the entire job!

Many of us have been taking this approach for years, on our countertops, on appliances, floors, walls, sinks, tubs, shower stalls, automobiles, and 400 other places. Hard soap crust on the bathroom sink where the soap sits can take several minutes of scrubbing, but if it is dampened first and given a chance to soften, it can be wiped off in seconds. Almost everything will clean *itself* with water and the right chemical. Water and a few cents' worth of chemicals can replace hours of your time when used according to the Universal Law of Cleaning.

Just apply the right solution and leave. Read. Rest! Apply more solution in another area, or do anything you want while the solution's chemical action loosens and suspends the dirt. Unless you get your kicks out of scrubbing, there's not much reason to scrape and grind soil off.

The Basic Principles of Cleaning

1. *Eliminate.* Sweep, dust-mop, brush, vacuum, or wipe all dirt, gravel, crumbs, and other loose debris from the surface.
2. *Saturate.* Apply cleaning solution generously to the dirty surface . . . and let it sit.

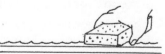

3. *Dissolve.* The liquid, and the chemical action of the cleaner, will loosen and dissolve the dirt.

4. *Remove.* With a sponge, cleaning cloth, or squeegee, remove the now-dissolved mushy dirt.

When people try to clean the grease and dust settled on top of their fridge they wipe the cleaning solution on—and often before it has time to break the gunk down and release it from the surface, they start scrubbing furiously. Let the solution do the work! By using the simple principle of eliminate, saturate, dissolve, remove in all cleaning, you can cut time and energy expenditure as much as we cut the floor job for the town recreation center.

On your house floors, for example, remove any forks, overshoes, yoyos, or dog bones and then sweep or dust mop the floor. Then mix up your cleaning solution and spread it on as large an area as you can handle before it dries out. As you're finishing at one end of the room, the solution you first laid down is working actively on the dirt, old wax, spots, stains, and marks. When you return to the first area and begin to mop or wipe it clean, the area you just left is now under heavy attack by the liquid, and most of the cleaning will have been accomplished by the time you get there with the mop.

This system will also work on heavier jobs like floor-stripping. When my sons and I cleaned the big floor in the village hall, we didn't spend a lot of time scrubbing. After dust-mopping, I spread the cleaning solution and ran over the surface with a floor machine (I could also have used a hand floor scrubber—see the equipment chart in Chapter 5). I didn't try to scrub or sand the floor clean; I went over it quickly to loosen the surface dirt so the chemical solution could do the work. By the time I reached the far end of the room, the solution spread on the first part had dissolved and suspended the dirty old wax. The next pass over the same area caused every drop of dirt and wax to come off. We squeegeed the floor with a floor squeegee (see the equipment chart in Chapter 5), picked up the gunk with a plain old dustpan, and put it in a bucket. (This eliminated the need for a "slop mop.") The floor was now clean, and we only needed to mop it with clear water. One mop bucket did the whole floor!

Less Is Best

When faced with a cleaning problem, always try to solve it with the gentlest cleaning solution or approach first. Don't call in a backhoe when a shovel will do. Aggressive cleaning methods may be necessary for very difficult situations, but they can also injure or destroy household furnishings and surfaces. As a cleaning product salesperson once put it, **"Only get as tough on a stain as the stain demands."** If rinsing with water will remove a stain, why start bleaching it? Don't reach for the heavy-duty cleaner until you've tried the all-purpose cleaner first. Don't scrub when you could soak. Don't scrape with a knife or razor until you've tried your fingernail first. Don't resort to a metal pot scrubber until first a white, then green nylon pad proves powerless. Less is best!

Abrasion Evasion

Using powdered cleansers and steel wool to grind dirt off surfaces has become a ritual for many home cleaners. With the same generosity used to apply powder to a baby's bottom, they coat their sinks with cleansing powder and attack them with brisk rubbing. You can actually hear the results as the grinding abrasion quickly removes stains and spots—along with some of the porcelain or chrome on the unit. The cleanser then has to be flushed off, and some of it will set like concrete in the gooseneck of the sink drain. The damage is gradual, but inevitable. On fiberglass or plastic sinks, tubs, and other fixtures, the damage isn't even gradual. Fiberglass isn't as tough as the old porcelain and enameled iron. It damages easily and, once damaged, is a pain to clean.

Even more important, you lose time cleaning by the abrasion method. You should be using the much quicker and easier cleaning principle *eliminate, saturate, dissolve, remove*. It really works. Always remember to use it, and you'll reward yourself with at least three-quarters of the time you once wasted grinding and scrubbing away!

Give the Solution Time to Work!

Whether you're cleaning a floor, wall, stovetop, tub, or patio, apply cleaning solution over as large an area as you can handle before it dries. Then let the chemical work. By the time you go back and wipe the area, the surface will for the most part have cleaned itself. If it doesn't come clean, reapply and wait a bit longer. How much time it takes the solution to deal with the dirt depends on how dirty the surface is. But let the solution do the work! It's a waste of time to concentrate on tiny areas and scrub.

Beware of Buildup!

In cases where all the dirt and wax won't quite come off and scrubbing seems called for, it's generally due to the lack of regular cleaning; a thick layer of wax and/or dirt has built up. Buildups of various kinds are the greatest obstacle to simple cleaning. The best example is that old villain: hard water. Look at the brand-new sparkling tile in your shower or at your exterior windows. They're going to get hard water on them from use, accidents, or splashes from our sinks and sprinklers.

Residue starts with an innocent drop. A drop doesn't seem much of a bother—unmolested, it will evaporate away . . . at least it will *appear* to leave. Closer examination reveals that each drop of water (in most parts of the country) contains something called mineral salts, which slide to the bottom of the drop as it evaporates. Though the drop appears to have vanished, a slight deposit of mineral salts remains. This is so subtle that it's ignored. Again water is splashed on the surface, new drops form in the place occupied by previous drops, and the new drops add their mineral marks to the existing residue. Six months, sixty showers, or twenty sprinklings later, that innocent first drop has become hard-water buildup.

If you remove hard water daily, or in many cases even weekly, it's a two-minute instead of a twenty-minute job. If you do it annually or "when I get around to it," it's a surface-damaging, chemical-squandering experience that greatly embitters one's attitude toward sanitation.

Grease Removal

Removing grease is something we're especially interested in once our hands start sticking to the stovetop or the cupboard doors. Grease buildup occurs indoors and out, as dirt is trapped and glued to things by airborne oils from cooking, heating, smoking, burning candles, auto emissions, etc. You'll struggle to clean greasy things if you don't use the right solution. Grease is acid, so you need a cleaner from the opposite end of the pH scale—an alkaline cleaner—to dissolve it. The more alkaline a cleaner, the more grease-cutting power it has. This is why ammonia, which has a high pH, works. A lot of heavy-duty cleaners on the market are designed to dissolve grease, and janitorial-supply stores sell "degreasers."

Here are two good ways to attack grease:

1. *For light degreasing:* Fill a spray bottle with a solution of heavy-duty cleaner. Spray it on and let it sit for about five minutes. Give the surfactants time to loosen, dissolve, and suspend the film of grease. Then wipe it dry with a cleaning cloth (see page 50). Ordinary hand dishwashing detergent is also good for light degreasing, since it is formulated to cut grease.

2. *For heavy degreasing:* Fill a bucket halfway with degreaser solution. Use a white-backed scrub sponge to apply a generous coat of the solution (not so much that it drips and runs) to the surface and let it sit on there for a while, up to fifteen minutes if necessary. Then scrub, rinse, and wipe dry to a luster with a cleaning cloth. If necessary, repeat the process.

When You Have to Scrub . . .

The right scrubbing tool is key. If you're cleaning something with deep crevices and textures, a stiff nylon brush will reach in and dig out the dirt. The brush should have a handle to keep your knuckles from getting scraped and your hands out of the dirt and chemicals. See the equipment chart in Chapter 5 for the type pro cleaners use.

For most other surfaces nothing beats nylon scrub pads. They have just the right degree of rub to remove rebellious residue, and they have more total contact with the surface than a brush does. The white nylon type can be used safely on most household surfaces—but even with these don't scrub too hard or too long on soft finishes such as plastic or latex paint. Use the more aggressive green nylon pads to remove more stubborn spots and deposits on nondelicate surfaces. The brown or black pads are too harsh for anything but wax stripping, concrete cleaning, and the like.

Always keep any surface you scrub wet. This aids the action and reduces the chance of damage and scratching. Add more solution when you need to so the surface doesn't dry as you work. If you use a brush, remember that brushes don't hold cleaning solution—you have to pour or spray the solution on first. Rinse the surface occasionally while you work, especially if it's textured or indented, to check on your progress and remove loosened soil.

Don't bear down on a brush when you use it—that actually lessens the cleaning action. If you doubt this, go get a brush out of the cabinet—any brush—and scrub lightly, daintily, with just a wee bit of pressure. Notice the points of the bristles are really massaging the heck out of things, loosening the soil and working the soap and solution in. Now press on the brush hard and notice how the bristles flatten. When you move the brush back and forth like this, the cleaning ends of the brush aren't doing a thing. The only parts of the brush hitting the surface are the sides of the bristles, which are smooth as a bundle of eels. When you add in the slipperiness of soap, that "cleaning action" isn't even tickling the surface!

I had a bristle brush under a 150-pound floor machine once, and my cleaning instructor told me to stick my hand under the edge of the brush. I thought it would rip my finger off, but the sides of the bristles gliding over my fingers were so smooth and slippery they didn't even clean my fingernails. Likewise, notice the next time you sweep a floor how a light stroke allows the bottoms of the bristles (where all the work is done) to contact the floor so they don't miss a sesame seed. Just as light taps of a hammer are usually more effective than a full hard swing, so it is with cleaning.

Keep Your Working Stuff Near You!

Some people claim you can walk eight to fifteen miles just doing a day of housework around the average house. I wouldn't doubt it; I used to walk one mile per room until I learned to keep my cleaning tools within reach. Too many people place their tools and buckets in a central "cleaning station" in the room and constantly walk three, four, even five or six steps back and forth during a project. They spend half of their time and energy traveling.

If you need the exercise, this central station method will work for you. But if you want to get the job done and have energy left for a tennis game or bowling or other personal sporting activity, figure out how to keep your tools (sponges, buckets, cloths, screwdriver, etc.) within your reach. For example, if you wash cupboards, set your tools on the counter instead of on the floor. Same with painting: If you hang the bucket on the ladder or hold it in your hand, it will save the bend and dip all the way to the floor and back up. Try it—you'll be amazed at the time and effort you save!

To keep your tools rounded up and ready at all times, to pick up and use and then put back away, a little plastic cleaning caddy or "maid basket" (kind of like a miniature janitor's cart) is hard to beat. Cleaning aprons sound good on paper, but they don't make much sense unless you clean steadily for several hours or so. They also make it hard to bend over, and you bump the walls as you work. Keep a caddy in every area that needs frequent cleaning, filled with whatever is needed to clean that area. Buy a bright color so you can see it easily and don't stumble over it or have to search for it.

Chapter Seven

More Professional Secrets for Home Cleaners

Since I wrote the first edition of this book more than twenty years ago now, I've constantly been asked—on radio and TV and at my seminars and in letters and e-mails—for more "secrets of the pros"; more things we professionals do that make a big difference in the time cleaning takes and in the quality of the results. So here is a whole chapter of more ways to make your cleaning life easier!

Outsmarting Interruptions

It's the same old frustrating story: You are right in the middle of something (and have a good head of steam) and someone knocks on the door, the phone rings, the kids start to shriek, you run out of supplies, something breaks, or you run across something you have to stop and deal with or handle. You might call them interruptions; I call them housework's number one enemy. Interruptions occur in every activity, but housework has such a humble status people may deem you unoccupied and think nothing of asking you to stop at their convenience. Life just won't go on hold while we clean. Here are three things you can do to control interruptions:

1. *Wield your mop at unpopular times!* Early, late, on holidays, during lunch—the times when everyone else is sleeping, playing, or eating. It's exactly like traffic time. You can go during the most popular to and from times (rush hours) and count on losing an hour to interruptions (stops and slowdowns)—or go a bit earlier or later or take a different route and cover the same miles in fifteen minutes. I can write or clean more from 5:00 to 8:00 a.m. than all the rest of the day put together, because there are no interruptions. Society, business, friends, relatives, and even kids close down at times. Find those times, and grab the bucket and run with it.

2. *Clean in short bursts.* Cleaning doesn't have to be one long session or a giant project. Some of the most efficient cleaning is done in short bursts, which add up to a lot of things done. Fifteen-minute time fragments are much harder to interrupt than a four-hour block of time that you've set aside. Even the busiest of us have small pieces of time available every day, and what are you doing with them now? If you just take advantage of the five, ten-, and fifteen-minute time fragments that fall your way every day, you may never have to spend all Saturday cleaning again. Take advantage of those TV commercials, phone calls that leave your hands free, waiting time, etc.

3. *Don't yield!* Simply say no. Most interruptions aren't mandatory, like so many of us think. Take the phone, for example: When it rings, many people run to get it as if they were possessed. Yet most of us haven't had more than one or two true emergency calls in our whole lives. One of my college professors used to say, "My life and

home isn't open to any fool with a dime." (Make that fifty cents or more now!)

When I'm right in the middle of pouring cement, or up on a ladder painting, and someone comes by or calls, stopping would be a real problem, so I don't. Or if I'm on a job where stopping and reassembling everything would double the work, I just keep on going. "But Don, it's Ms. Éclair from *Toothpaste Today*" (like God calling). Well, if she were in the middle of writing an editorial, I wouldn't expect her to break her concentration and drop everything to talk to me. So I'll call her back.

Here's a little secret about interruptions: Once you refuse to lay out your life and time at will to family, friends, and passing salespeople, they'll begin to adjust their timetables and curb their impositions on you. **You are the one who sets the mood for the amount of meddling in your schedule.** You can control it. You don't need to force people to make an appointment with you for everything, but you can demand appreciation of the value of your time—it works.

When Is the Best Time to Clean?

We are all growing more and more aware of time, and ever more short of it.

Finding the time to clean in a world busy with "better" things to do *is* a big question—especially since cleaning doesn't usually top our list of "exciting things to do today." When I started looking at when I clean and at others who seemed to have the cleaning problem licked, I noticed that none of us clean in prime time. A lot of us can't because we work outside the home during what we think of as "prime time"—but *not* cleaning during prime time is my philosophy anyway.

When we feel good and are really rolling on some other project, stopping to clean means stopping to do something that someone else is just going to mess up again, anyway. It produces resentment in us all. When you have momentum elsewhere, that's just not the time to stop and spit-polish a house—even if things are dirty and you've scheduled it— because you'll hate every minute of it.

Cleaning isn't hard, nor does it require maximum physical or mental powers—so when body and spirit are in a lull or at loose ends, when you're not doing much anyway, *that's* when you should jump in and clean. It's stimulating, good exercise, and best of all, you'll know you're not squandering your most precious time to do it. So it's almost like getting free time.

If you clean when you're running out of energy you'll get a mental second wind and even a physical boost—cleaning can actually be a way of recharging yourself. And since cleaning doesn't take your full attention, you can do other things while you clean that refresh your mind and spirit, so you almost get "double duty" out of the time. For instance:

1. *Note and create.* Carry a pad and pencil with you and jot down ideas, impressions, things you suddenly see or understand while shoveling away at dirt and clutter. Some of our best thoughts and inspirations come during half-attention times, and cleaning is certainly one of those. I've often written more creative things in half an hour of cleaning than in half a day at the keyboard.

2. *Rhapsodize.* You can listen to music, and then you can *listen* to music—truly hear and savor it. When most of us listen to music our minds are too occupied to pay much attention. When you clean, music can really raise the goosebumps, because cleaning doesn't take much concentration and it really benefits from a rhythm backup.

3. *Teach the family.* How many opportunities are left in the world to teach children the basic principles of cooperation and responsibility? A hundred years ago most

Americans lived in rural areas, and parents were with their children all day, week after week, sharing chores. Today about 5 percent of us are down on the farm, and the rest of us hunt and strain to find experiences and challenges to share with our family. Cleaning is one of the few things left. You can formally sit down a fourteen-year-old and lecture about the value of self-esteem and discipline . . . or visit and converse while you clean together.

4. *Daydream.* Daydreaming is not just soothing—it's a source of endless ideas. When you're preparing a presentation, operating a machine at a construction site, or doing anything that takes your full attention—including driving—daydreaming is an inefficient, if not dangerous, thing to do. But with cleaning, you've done it all before—you know how to handle the vacuum, the squeegee, the sponge—so you can click into your "wouldn't this be a great world if" mode as you sail through the soap scum.

5. *Focus on the rewards.* When you start on a room, deciding how to clean it is just reflex—how neat and inviting it'll look when you're through is what you should really focus on. Even those stove rings that are so slow to surrender the burned-on-crud—imagine those as the shining halos they'll be when you're done! Weird, maybe, but it works! Remember, all rewards don't come from life's fun and play activities; most of them come from the tough and responsible things you do.

A few more rewards for us cleaners: Satisfaction—that you used your skill and the result was good. Pride—it sits there looking great and you know you did it. Relief—it's finally done and you won't have to do it again for a while!

What Can I Do with the Kids While I Clean?

This is one of the few cleaning problems I haven't solved. You can't put off cleaning until the kids are in college. You learn to clean around their schedule as long as you have to. The baby will boggle you, the teens try you, the grandkids grind down all thought of ever conquering cleaning with kids. But kids actually mold some of the world's best cleaners, giving them eternal surprises and only fragments of time to handle them in. Here are a few ways to lengthen your leash:

- Most of the principles of interruption prevention (see pages 70 to 71) will work with kids—especially the off-hours approach. When they're down or on nap idle, watch how quickly and cheerfully (and quietly) we clean!
- Shift the overseeing of the younger set to your mate for the occasion: "One of us does the floors and one of us does the kids. You pick."
- Send the kids to the neighbors' house to play. (You can return the favor later in the week when they're trying to clean.)
- Hire a babysitter for a few hours a couple of days a week, or make arrangements with a nearby preschool. Or you might just decide to spend the money on a housekeeper (see pages 86-88). Grandparents are great at watching kids while you clean (and they don't mind feeling genuinely needed either).
- When you don't have the kids, do as much "cleaning as you go" as you can. Clean the shower while you shower, the tub as the water goes down the drain, etc.
- A very young child, as long as he's not wet or hungry, should be happy to watch you sweep or fold laundry for a while from a portable baby seat, cradle, playpen, or baby "corral" set on the floor nearby—especially if you keep up

a lively dialogue or have on some peppy music. There are also nice portable battery-powered baby swings.

- Set up a play area in a basement or other room if the kids are old enough to be alone. Promise a special reward if they remain in the area until you're done. (Use a kitchen timer to let them see how much time remains.)

- Carefully chosen light chores (such as dusting with a lambswool duster or spot cleaning) can be done with a baby nestled in a carrier across your chest. Baby back-packs leave your hands freer, but they're less safe since you can't see what's going on back there.

- If all else fails, go for a good movie or compelling computer game.

- Let them help! Even after raising six of our own and leading Scout troops and church youths numbering into the hundreds, I continue to be amazed at how much work a kid can do. By the age of eight—the official age of accountability—kids can do almost anything as well as adults. And you tell me something better for kids to do while you clean . . . than help clean!!

No Sweat . . . and Little Strain

The wonderful thing about watching professionals perform is that they always make what they do seem effortless. Just remember, when you see pro window cleaners squeegeeing an acre of glass at a stretch, they do that every day and you don't. Try to imitate it, and you can quickly get sore and even injured. How can you keep cleaning casualties at a minimum?

Get Help

Few of us get hurt doing regular housework. It's that "spring" cleaning campaign, the once-a-year effort and strain, that has the greatest possibility of leaving you with an ache or pain. It's always that giant reach or heavy lift that we justify by saying to ourselves, "It's only this once." That's all it takes. When is anything large or cumbersome moved upstairs or down, for example, without smashed fingers, chipped finishes, or grazed walls? An object doesn't have to be superheavy—"awkward" is enough to put undue strain on the spine, and back injuries are the number one cause of medical claims in the cleaning industry. After years of seeing even professional cleaners get hurt in such situations I have one directive to know and live by: *Get help.* Even the most fit man or woman needs help sometimes. Two people reduce the weight and risk by half, and three is even better. Help will speed things up too.

Reduce Bending and Reaching.

"Never trust a maid with clean knees," they used to say. That was probably true in great-grandma's day, but today if you get your knees dirty cleaning, you aren't doing it right. Bending is tiring and it gets old faster than we do. **Minimizing bending and reaching is the secret of fast, tireless cleaning.** So ask, "How can I put a handle on this?" of every cleaning operation you come across.

Use a long-handled floor scrubber (see the equipment chart in Chapter 5) for all those chores you used to do on hands and knees. You can also use a long-handled floor scrubber to clean things like shower walls, grimy outside windows, and house siding.

Extension handles (see page 55) make any high reach a cinch and keep your feet on the ground. Extension poles can be used on lambswool dusters and paint rollers as well as squeegees. And they can be used to extend your reach down as well as up.

Another way to reduce reaching is to get a taller ladder or have someone hold the ladder and hand things to you.

Lift the Right Way

When lifting (even light things) up from the floor, lift with your legs. Let yourself down to the level of the object with your leg muscles, rather than bending over it with your back. After you have a good grip, use your leg muscles to lift you and the object back up.

Use the Right-Sized Tools

In all your cleaning tools, get the right size. Ever try hiking in a shoe that doesn't fit? That's about where you are with a tool that's too big or too little for the job at hand. Buy buckets, sponges, handles, vacuums, etc., to fit you and your cleaning chores. Or adjust or whittle them to fit if you have to.

Forget about oversized buckets. You won't be able to lift them when they're full, and you'll slop, spill, and strain yourself trying. If you clean with a two-bucket system (see page 128), you won't need more than two quarts of cleaning solution, anyway.

What's the Best Direction to Clean?

1. *Top to bottom:* When you dust, start at the top and work down, and do the same when you wash walls.
2. *North and south, east and west:* When you scrub anything, go in four directions—first north and south, then east and west. That's because almost everything—even seemingly flat surfaces such as concrete or vinyl—has a grain or texture, even if you might need a magnifying glass to see it. When you scrub in circles, you really only clean and massage one side of that texture. When you scrub back and forth, you only get two sides. When you go in all four directions you agitate even the tiniest protrusions and pores and loosen the dirt more quickly and effectively.

And you're far less likely to miss places. You'll find this makes a big difference in all kinds of cleaning.

3. *Back to front:* If you clean a room from back to front (toward the door), you save steps because you walk through the room just once and then work your way back out. If you clean in the other direction, you walk through the room at least twice and probably more.

4. *Clockwise:* Cleaning your way around a room clockwise is another efficient approach. You might prefer to work counterclockwise, toward the left—the important thing is to start in one direction and keep going that way.

Switch-Hitting

Most people are either right- or left-handed and do most of their work with that hand. Switch-hitting batters are able to swing from either side of the plate, so they can instantly adjust to either a right-or left-handed pitcher. Switch-hitting gives you an edge in cleaning, too. Once you're really rolling on something, the longer you can keep it up, the better off you are. Once you pick up the duster, dust it all. Once the broom is in your hand, sweep it all. You get in a kind of rhythm this way, and it's a lot faster than stopping and restarting forty times in one afternoon. So when one arm gets tired, switch to the other and don't stop. It'll be awkward at first, but if you can learn to do it you can pick up hours in a day of work.

"Holidays" or Misses

Despite years of athletic training in my youth, there's one move I've never mastered: leaning way over a newly waxed floor, scanning and squinting to see if I missed a place. After the applicator is rinsed and hung to dry, the wax bottle put away, and all the furniture is back in place, finding a flat or dull spot on the floor can ruin the whole job, as well as your ego.

These places we miss with mops, paint rollers, brushes, or wax applicators are what the professionals call "holidays." How do we avoid them? Cross the area twice for total coverage, and then once more for security. **Whether you're cleaning, painting, or waxing, pass over every surface at least three times.** Do this and your work will never go on a holiday. The extra passes take half the time it takes to crane your neck enough to spot all the misses you'll make in a fast single pass.

Give Yourself a Janitor Closet

Even the best cleaning supplies won't do much good if you can't find them when you need them. Since most homes don't have a janitor closet or any respectable space for cleaning materials, you need to engineer your own storage space. First, about 70 percent of the cleaning stuff under the average kitchen sink is only used once a year, if that. Dejunk this antique collection down to the things you really use. Then get a plastic caddy. Put what you need for the sink area in the caddy, and if you don't have small children you can even leave the caddy under the sink. Working from a caddy, you won't set acid or corrosive cleaners on household surfaces and leave rings and burns. Keep a similar caddy of supplies anywhere else you clean frequently.

For the big stuff—brooms, mops, buckets, squeegees, the vacuum and its attachments—preempt a closet, perhaps near the kitchen, and even if you have to remove shelves to do it, make yourself a cleaning center. Suspend all you can off the floor—hang brooms, mops, and brushes by their handles on sturdy hooks (so they can get enough air circulation to dry fast and won't warp out of shape). Be sure you hang a treated dust mop, too (see page 121). If you lean it against the wall or leave it flat on the floor, the oil will wick out and may leave a stain. Keep cleaning chemicals on an eye-level shelf (safely out of youngsters' reach) with the labels turned toward you. Keep dangerous cleaning chemicals, pesticides, and even plastic bags on one or two high shelves. Use wire racks or bins if you have room to mount anything; they allow air circulation so stored cloths and sponges can dry quickly. After you clean off your scrub pads and squeegee, drop them into the bucket you use them with, so they're easy to find and all ready to carry off to the cleaning site.

Don't allow any squatters here, either. If your rug shampooer is seldom used, store it neatly in the garage.

Dress for Success

First, you never want to clean barefoot. Stay away from your best shoes, high heels, and sandals. You're on your feet a lot when you clean, so wear shoes or boots with good support and traction tread (and to live to clean another day, go for rubber soles when working on wet floors). Athletic shoes or sneakers are excellent because they're light, yet sure-footed. Trying to clean in those old, tired slippers will fatigue you fast and greatly increase your chance of tripping and slipping.

You don't have to clean in your workout clothes, but I do recommend that you wear loose comfortable clothing such as sweatpants and a T-shirt. It's tough to stretch and bend in tight jeans or skirts. I always like to wear a long-sleeved shirt and leave the shirttails out when I clean. This saves your arms from scratches and burns, and any dead spiders that fall will end up on the floor, not in your pants. (P.S. If you look neat and attractive while you clean, you'll feel better about it!)

Rubber gloves are a cleaner's best friend—use them when you need to. They protect your skin from harsh chemicals, protect your nails from grime and breakage, and keep your hands out of yucky, germy messes. Long contact with even mild chemicals can dry out your hands, and some of the more toxic ones will not merely irritate or burn your skin but be absorbed right through it. Get good latex gloves with a comfortable flocked lining. Use one size bigger than your hand size for easy on and off.

Safety glasses were invented to protect you from splashes of acids or strong alkaline chemicals, especially if you're working above your head. If in doubt, don't go without—it's not worth the chance of losing your eyesight. (And no, regular glasses aren't just as good.)

Cleaning You Can Cut Back On

Remember as a kid, when someone "did you dirty," you snubbed the person and made believe you didn't know he or she was there? We all did it, and it was a bad thing to do to people. But it's not at all a bad approach to some of our cleaning chores. Lots of us clean innocent things that don't really need it. Many times I've been led through a home to look at a tub, floor, or fixture that won't come clean, and I've been amazed. The thing would have lasted thirty years, but it was on the way out after only ten, because it was worn out from all the cleaning. We all know an Annie Septic or Sam Overshine who does this. You could call it

overkill, and plenty of us do it because we feel guilty if we don't clean things regularly.

The outdoors is largely paved today, so we don't track in half the mud, gravel, dirt, and straw they did in Grandpa's day. Modern homes with better weather stripping, carpeted floors and entryways, and fewer cracks and holes around windows and doors let in less dirt and dust. Soot and smoke from heating was a big problem thirty years ago, too, and it's almost eliminated today.

When I was in college, my cleaning crew and I often had five homes a day to clean. We had faithful clients who always called us for their annual big cleaning—washing down every wall and ceiling, shampooing all the carpet, cleaning all the windows, even painting. As their children grew up and left home, the housekeeping load was lighter, but out of habit they'd still call us to do "spring cleaning" that could have gone undone. Sometimes my cleaning water would be clear as a glass of 7 Up after cleaning three rooms! "We can't find any dirt," I'd tell the owners. And they'd say, "But Don, it's been a year. . . . " You can go months without doing windows and vacuuming in certain places. Too many people think they have a moral obligation to do things "every day" or "once a week" or "once a month."

The following are a few tasks you could trim back on, and relieve yourself both of cleaning effort and a guilty conscience:

- **Windows:** No matter how dirty glass gets, it doesn't rot or get ruined (except perhaps by heavy hard-water deposits). It won't hurt anything to slack off on cleaning windows—although they might give you a little visual pain (pun intended!). Besides, as long as you're not confronted with it close up (such as on the top of a coffee table), even dirty glass gives the illusion of clean.
- **Vacuuming:** An important procedure, to be sure, but only regularly necessary in the traffic patterns. Lint under

furniture and on the edges of the carpet doesn't hurt a thing, so the rest of the carpet can be done semimonthly or even less. Meanwhile, a hand vac can catch those few dust balls or cookie crumbs.

- **Closets:** When it comes to actual cleaning (walls, floors, ceilings), closets just don't get dirty, although they do need to be dejunked every so often. You might want to occasionally sweep or damp-wipe the floor in a closet. It's a good idea to clean the closets once if you're moving into an older home, but forget them for at least the next decade.

- **Ceilings:** People seem to clean the ceiling every time they do the walls, which is really overkill. Ceilings just don't get the same fingerprints and bumps that walls do, so leave them until about every third or fourth time (except for kitchen ceilings, which do get greasy and may need to be cleaned more often). If dirt buildup around a heat register mars a section of a ceiling, just clean the buildup around the vent—don't feel like you have to do the whole thing.

- **Pits:** We all own something with a pitted or indented surface (generally a floor), and it drives us crazy trying to get it really clean. This is a flaw in the design, not in your cleaning prowess, so don't let it get you down. If the dirt doesn't lift out or dissolve away with one or two passes of a scrub brush, then leave it and call it shading. No one will know. When the dirt fills in to the top of the pits, call it a "design correction." (You can also alleviate a flooring pit problem by filling the pits with wax after a good cleaning.)

- **Silverware:** Why do people polish silverware and then put it away, just so they can take it out and polish it again? When they're busy feeding their faces, most people won't notice whether it's stainless steel or sterling, anyway.

- **Carpet shampooing:** Professional matting inside and out at every entrance and regular vacuuming of traffic areas will do a lot to delay the need for shampooing. You have to judge when to do it, but don't shampoo every year just because that's the schedule. Your home may only need it every two or three years. My wife and I went ten years in one new house without shampooing the carpet, and we had a big, active family and many guests, and owned hundreds of pro carpet shampooers, with some stored right on the premises.

- **Cobwebs:** These aren't the ultimate index of housework neglect—they can appear overnight. You could argue that they actually aid cleaning by trapping dust and airborne grease along with the bugs. A daily cobweb safari isn't necessary, and if a cobweb freaks out a guest, be sure to thank the person for spotting it for you.

- **Inside the cupboards:** Most of us could get by honorably for ten or twenty years just wiping out the bottom of the shelves, but some people empty the entire cupboard every year to wash or paint . . . it's unnecessary.

- **Towel washing:** You can use a towel for a week before it's actually dirty (remember, you only dry yourself with towels, after you're already clean). Who needs four towels per person per week, including one so big you drag it on the floor trying to dry yourself? Why not save lots of water and washing time?

- **Bathrooms:** Okay, there may be a toilet in there, but bathrooms are actually one of the most sanitary places in a home. Ninety percent of a bathroom is hard surfaces such as tile, porcelain, and metal, which don't absorb dirt. And when we're in there, we're usually washing ourselves. If you don't clean the bathroom constantly you won't disgrace yourself or endanger your family.

- **Interior chrome and stainless steel:** These are usually water spotted, not dirty. It's nice to have gleaming chrome, but your guests would probably rather focus on you than the coffee table frame. As for trying to keep chrome faucets unspotted—why try to create the impression they're never used?

- **Brass and copper:** Anything made of brass or copper can either be left to develop a handsome natural patina, or laboriously detarnished every couple of months so that they can develop a new coat of tarnish that will have to be removed again. Which makes more sense?

- **Furniture polishing:** No, you don't have to pour or blast a puddle of polish onto every piece of furniture every week—or even every month. Applying too much oil or wax to furniture may look good briefly, but it creates a sticky, gummy mess in the end.

- **Drying dishes:** Guess what—letting them drip-dry in the drainer isn't just easier, it's more hygienic.

Speaking of sanitation, frenetic oversanitizing of ordinary household surfaces and areas is another practice worth examining. There are times and places when it's needed, but also many reasons not to do it otherwise: Overuse of antibacterial products can worsen the growing problem of antiseptic-resistant microbes; research has shown that children and adults raised around a little ordinary household and garden dirt are actually healthier; it's also hard to truly disinfect household surfaces by the ordinary means used by home cleaners, so much of this may be a waste of time anyway.

If it hasn't been used and it isn't dirty, don't clean it just because it's there. You don't need to relax your cleaning standards, just re-examine them. Cleaning to make things sparkly instead of just giving them a healthy glow is often a waste of time and effort. What in the name of life and love is of more value—germ fighting or heart-lighting?

Call in a Pro

When things get out of hand, when you're in over your head, when there's just too much on the agenda—get help. That's what the professionals do, and they're never ashamed to do it. There are more than 100,000 cleaning companies and maid services in the United States. Even where there isn't an official licensed cleaning firm, there are dependable individuals who clean house on a regular basis (which many people in fact prefer over "big company" service).

Just as housework is often more than whisking up a bit of dust and adjusting an off-center lamp, so is there a difference in the types of professional people you can hire. Many maid services are essentially a sort of skim service. They often won't do any of the heavy housework, like cleaning outside windows, ovens, or carpets, washing walls or stripping and waxing floors. They may do these "big jobs" for a special hourly rate, but usually they just scoot in and dust, vacuum, make beds, straighten, touch up, and go.

Maid services charge by the house or by the visit. Should you use a franchised service or an independent? Independents have both more to gain and more to lose by pleasing or not pleasing you. **Think about what the services offered are actually worth to you, not only in terms of cost but in terms of time freed for other things.** How many hours of help, how many times a week or month, does your household need to prevent minor chores from backing up?

Hire a maid service on a trial basis to begin with. You might have to go through a few to get the maid you like and trust, but give it a while and you'll find someone reliable who works at reasonable a rate. When you find somebody good, talk to him or her about returning weekly, monthly, or whatever. You need service you can count on, and if those you hire know they'll be getting regular work they can give you a better price, and probably better service.

Professional cleaners (as opposed to maid services) are the people equipped to do the big, hard jobs calling for big, heavy equipment. Call pro cleaners when you have a major, one-time or seasonal job.

Picking a Real Pro

You're the only one who can decide when and if you need or want a professional to do your cleaning. But the cleaning business has a high turnover and failure rate. When you decide to go outside, how do you make sure you pick the right professional? Following are some guidelines from someone who knows the business inside out:

- *Don't just believe all the claims on the brochure.* Get references and actually check them. Sure, they'll always give their best, but some are better than none. Remember that you'll probably want to use this person or outfit for years. They'll be in your house and around your children and valuables, so taking the time to check them out with a few phone calls or letters is well worth it—just as if you were picking a doctor for surgery. Finding out whom your well-satisfied friends or neighbors use to do their cleaning can save you some detective work.

- *Ask how long they've been in business.* Anyone who's been around less than a couple of years would make me nervous. If someone lasts in this business more than three years, they're generally worth a try.

- *Get a bid.* Anyone who knows the business knows what a given job involves and can give you a bid—not merely an estimate, but an actual price. Have them spell out what they will do, when, and how much it will cost. If someone says they won't, can't, or don't know, they shouldn't get a foot in your house to experiment. Most real professionals have a form that fits all of this and a place for them, you, or both to sign. Get it in writing, and hold them to it.

- *Never, never pay in advance.* Professional cleaners have very little upfront expenses (only 6 percent of the cost of a cleaning job is materials and supplies), so paying in advance is neither necessary nor wise.

- *Get proof of insurance.* We never feel we should have to worry about such things, but an accident that happens on your premises to someone without professional insurance can easily end up your problem. This is one reason you contract work, so the pro will furnish the skill, the muscles, and the tools, and assume the liabilities. The cleaners you want will not only be insured but bonded as well. Remember, however, that even if they do have insurance it doesn't protect the contents of your home. If they ruin a couch cleaning it, they're not insured for workmanship, generally just liability—another reason to choose wisely the people who will be within your walls.

- *Find out who will come on the job.* It's seldom the sharp, clean-cut person who gives the bid. Too often the ones who show up are surly, fresh recruits, and you may end up having to train them. Once a contractor knows you expect and demand the best, that's generally what you'll get.

Chapter Eight
Prevention: Keeping the Enemy Out

What do we do with the dirt on the farm?
It flies from the road and comes straight from the barn.
It pours through the windows and tracks on the floors.
We give up and just plant our garden indoors.

—Marilyn May

Mats: a Must

A new hospital, nestled in a valley with one of the world's most famous ski resorts, had been in operation for two years when its housekeeping personnel retired. Replacements were needed and a professional cleaning service was contracted. Following careful measurement of the space, occupancy, and conditions, and after interviews with the retiring staff members, it was concluded that twelve hours of work was required each night to clean the offices, public area, entrances, and medical administrative wing. When signing the contract, the owner of the janitorial company made one explicit request: both entrances to the hospital were to be covered with vinyl-backed nylon mats running at least 15 feet inside both entrances. There had been no mats before, because it was thought they might detract from the hospital's alpine beauty. The hospital's administrator agreed to order the doormats that day.

The cleaning company began its service and was spending twelve hours plus a few extra daily to keep the place up to standard. They wet-mopped nightly, used six treated dust-control cloths on the floor, and had to scrub some areas every week with their floor machines. Anticipating the difference the new mats would make, the cleaning company owner had the sweeping and vacuuming crew keep track of residue collected from the floors throughout the building. Each night a gallon can was half-filled with gravel, sand, thread, pine needles, and every other thing common to a resort area. Three weeks later,

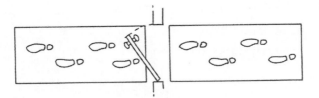

For best results, both interior and exterior mats should be at least four strides long,

the mats arrived and were installed at both entrances.

The first night the mats were in place, the hours of work dropped to ten, and the sweeping residue was reduced to half a quart of gum wrappers, toothpicks, etc. After one week, the new mats reduced the cleaning to nine hours per night. The dust cloths were reduced from six to two, wet mopping was reduced to twice a week, and dusting to every other night. Cleaning supplies were cut by more than 50 percent. The mats were paid for in less than one week in labor and cleaning supplies saved. The hospital also noted that fewer people slipped and fell at the entrances, and the mats lasted for four years!

Proper matting alone can save the average household approximately 200 hours of work a year, slow down structural depreciation, and save as much as $100 in cleaning supplies. The cost of matting for the average home is about $150 to $200. But the 200 hours is big savings for you. That's thirty minutes a day cut from chore time.

The reasons for such savings are easy to understand if you simply ask yourself, "What is it that I clean out of my house, off my rugs and hard floors, off the walls, off the furniture, etc.?" Dust and dirt are the obvious answers. Where does it come from? Most of it comes from the outside. How does it get inside? Eighty percent of it is *transported* in (the rest leaks through cracks, is airborne, or originates inside). A five-person home accumulates forty pounds of dust and dirt a year—dust composed of everything from air pollution particles and top-soil to dead insects and pet dander, and dirt carried into the home via clothes and feet.

Professionals estimate that it costs hundreds of dollars per pound to remove dirt once it's inside the house. It costs *you* even more in time:

1. You vacuum carpets more often, and shampoo them because of that dirt embedded in them.
2. You sweep and dust-mop hard floors more often, and strip and wax the floor because of that dirt embedded in it.
3. You change furnace and air conditioner filters more often and dust, dust, dust because of that dirt circulating in the air.
4. You wash clothes more often because of that dirt.
5. Your cleaning equipment and supplies are used up and wear out faster because of that dirt.

Proper matting will:

1. Keep your house cleaner
2. Reduce the need for sweeping, vacuuming, dusting, mopping, shampooing, and waxing
3. Absorb sound
4. Enhance safety
5. Improve the overall appearance of your home

All this saves you both time and money. It takes one piece of equipment and a few minutes to get dirt out of a mat. It takes ten pieces of equipment and hours to get it out of your home!

Where is your carpet the dirtiest? At the entrance, in about a 3-by-4-foot area, where the matting should be. It's only logical—if dirt doesn't get in, you won't have to round it up. As a person criticizing mats once said, "Bah! I hate doormats—all they are is dirt catchers!" I rest my case.

Taking advantage of good matting is the smartest, easiest, and least expensive thing you can do to cut your housecleaning time. It's easier to vacuum or shake out a mat than it is to chase dirt all over the house. Think about the hospital example. The dirt and debris distributed throughout it daily were reduced from a half gallon to one pint.

Mats will perform a great service in your home. Don't take my word for it—try it! You'll cry over the lost years of labor and money you've wasted by not getting adequate mats sooner. Instead of scrubbing your floor weekly, you could end up doing it annually. (I've even had one commercial building go *five years*, and the floor finish still looked good.)

If you have good matting, all the fine gravel, grit, and dirt that hangs on the bottoms of shoes and scratches and soils things will be out of action. Any kind of floor will last a long time when it isn't abused by grit. Next time you go into an office building, notice the difference in the floor on the lower level as compared to the upper-level floors. Even if the traffic is the same, the upper ones will last twice as long and look twice as good because the grit doesn't get to them. Traffic doesn't hurt a floor much—it's the abrasiveness of dirt that creates havoc. Keep it out of your home, and you'll keep yourself out of the crouching, scrubbing position. That's the sensible way to clean house—not to have to do it in the first place!

How to Mat an Entrance

Use professional-quality nylon, olefin, or polypropylene mats with vinyl or rubber backing inside and synthetic-grass (AstroTurf) mats outside. These mats are available in a wide range of colors and can be obtained in rolls or in precut sizes at a janitorial-supply house. For best results, the mats should be at least four strides long each.

Some Mats to Sidestep

Avoid decorative mats. We all love to see our name in print—even on a rubber doormat. But a mat like this doesn't do much good, and the time it takes to clean around it is probably greater than the cleaning time it saves. Link mats (the kind made from little slices of old car tires wired together) are ineffective for most homes and extremely dangerous for wearers of high heels. Coco mats are more trouble than they're worth because they don't absorb well and they shed. Have you ever tried to clean a coco mat? That alone should convince you not to buy one!

Following are some matting pointers that will advance your goal of gaining thirty free minutes a day:

Avoid using leftover carpet squares.
Don't use mats without nonskid backing.
Get rid of link or perforated mats.

For outside the house, the synthetic-grass-type mats such as AstroTurf or any rough-textured, unperforated mat with a rubber back is good. These won't rot, they're easy to clean, and they'll knock the big stuff off the shoes or boots of the person coming into your home. Try to get a mat at least 5 feet long so that people entering your home will have to take three or four steps on it. The exact type of exterior mat to buy depends on the space available, overhead cover (awning or porch), and your home and landscaping style.

Mats for Inside the House, Too

The first thing you need to do is get rid of any carpet samples or scraps you're using for "throw rugs." These items are appropriately named. The jute backing and curling edges can throw their users into the hospital. They're unsafe, unattractive, and—more to the point—inefficient. Get rid of them!

To Maintain Mats

1. Keep them vacuumed.
2. When they're dirty, hose them down, apply some all-purpose cleaner solution, scrub a bit, and hose them again.
3. Squeegee off excess water with a floor squeegee or old window squeegee.
4. Hang mats to dry. Never use them when the back is wet.

At any janitorial-supply store, you can buy professional-quality vinyl or rubber-backed nylon, olefin, or polypropylene mats for inside your home. This type of mat helps to reduce falls and traps loose dirt—the same dirt you'd be cleaning from everything in the house. They are efficient, will last up to fifteen years, and are available in a wide variety of colors. They come in widths of 3 or 4 feet, and in any length. The fibers of these types of mat create a static charge that actually helps pull particles from your shoes and clothes. The mats will also absorb mud and water from foot traffic and hold it in their roots. They won't show dirt easily and can be vacuumed like any other carpet.

Some mats will creep a little on some surfaces, and a "rug hugger" type with a textured back can be purchased if you get tired of retrieving the carpet. Or you can get polyester "sticky pads" or "grip strips" from a hardware or janitorial-supply store to keep mats from creeping or bunching.

An often-forgotten area in our homes that should also be well matted is the garage entrance, if you have a garage. Plenty of sawdust, oil stains, and project residue get tracked into the house from the garage. Fine silt, sand, and gravel often get caught up in the snow that lodges under a car and falls loose on the garage floor. When it melts, the sand and grit are carried into the house by foot. Concrete dust and garage-type soils and dirt are abrasive to carpet as well as hard flooring.

You Need Mats Even if You Don't Have a House!

Apartments, condominiums, mobile homes, and motor homes need to be matted, too. The smaller amount of dirt and debris that might get to the upper floor of an apartment building is multiplied by the fact that the gritty city dirt has a smaller area over which to distribute itself—hence the soiling and damage to the dwelling can be as acute as in a large, dust-surrounded farmhouse.

It takes one piece of equipment and a few minutes to get dirt out of a mat. It takes ten pieces of equipment and hours to get it out of your home.

A 3 × 5-foot mat is an excellent all-purpose size. It's wide enough for the average doorway, long enough that people entering your home will have to take three or four steps on it, and light enough to handle and to clean easily.

An extra 3 × 12-foot runner can be rolled up and kept for remodeling, parties, or wet weather. This extra mat will be a good investment if your traffic, lifestyle, or location merits it. It would be an especially good idea for a newly built home, since it's common for a family to move in before the landscaping is completed. The several months of working on the yard generates a lot of mud, and the resulting damage is often unnoticed because the house is new.

Not only will you save thirty minutes a day when you install adequate matting, but your doorways and entrances will be better looking, quieter, and safer. Get mats before you start to clean, and you won't have to start as soon or work as long.

Other Preventive Measures

Now that you have your mats lying in wait for all that creeping dirt, you ought to set up a few more culprit catchers for the things that cause housework. Remember again, the idea isn't to get faster, bigger, or better tools to beat the dirt. The first principle of cleaning is not to have to do it in the first place.

Cure Litter

Make it a hard and fast rule in your home that everyone picks up his or her own litter and is responsible for personal belongings. And make it relatively simple for everyone to abide by the rule. Provide trash containers for every room in the house, as well as outside where the kids play. Empty the containers frequently, before the contents become attractive to germs, insects, and larger animals.

Make sure there are enough shelves, drawers, racks, hooks, and toy boxes for everyone to put away belongings quickly and easily. If there's a place to put it, chances are much better that it'll end up where it ought to (rather than on the couch, the bed, the floor, or the stairs).

> The trouble with cleaning up litter is that when you're finished, you're right where you should have been before you started!

Prepare

Putting a cover over or under anything that needs protection when you clean, paint, etc., will save all kinds of unnecessary cleaning. We're always tempted to skip this little step and we always pay for it later—with a lot of extra work, if not with ruined objects. So get out those tarps, drop cloths, or old newspapers and use them.

Get It Out of the Dirt Zone

What's up and out of the way won't have to be cleaned, and that's the name of the prevention game. So make sure all your unused but needed stuff is hung or in a cupboard, out of the way of daily traffic that will soil and abuse it.

> Wrinkles: a condition of creased, crinkled, and crumpled that we get with age, and our possessions get when not folded or hung carefully. A little prevention can save a lot of ironing.

Animals

There's no getting around the fact that house animals create housework and cause damage, but you can minimize it. If you do have an indoor/outdoor pet, consider installing a pet door so it can come in and go out at will. This saves wear and tear on the people door if your pet's a scratch-at-the-door type (and it saves you from being the animal's doorperson). Use a disinfectant cleaner when you clean up after animals.

Both cats and dogs should be brushed regularly and their claws trimmed. Your vet can show you how to do this. Dogs should be bathed as soon as they start smelling "doggy." An inexpensive pet rake will be a big help in coping with shedding hair (see the equipment chart in Chapter 5).

Vacuum pet hair off upholstered furniture. Better yet, keep animals off furniture, or designate one chair that's belongs to them and keep a throw cover over it that you can wash easily.

Build your cat a good scratching post. Make sure it's tall enough for the cat to stretch full length, and weight the base so the cat can't tip it over. If you cover it with carpeting, use the loopy kind that will engage the cat's claws. A harsh, scratchy surface like woven sisal, or even highly textured fabric like burlap, is better than carpeting of any kind.

Pet problems can often be traced to problems with the training process. It's important to spend as much time training your pets as you do loving them. This will reduce pet accidents to a minimum. **After you train your pets, make sure that you're trained, too.** If you're too tired to change that litter box or take your dogs out to relieve themselves, then you have to take the credit for the puddle on your carpet. Pets try to please you. But when they can't wait any longer, it happens. Pets demand responsibility. Don't allow your pets (and your household furnishings) to suffer for lack of it.

For a complete guide to a cleaner coexistence with indoor pets, see my book *Pet Clean-Up Made Easy, 2nd Edition*.

Mildew

Mildew looks bad and can be damaging, but it isn't really a cleaning problem. Mildew is a fungus that thrives on moisture and temperatures between 75° and 85°F. There are five ways to help prevent mildew growth:

1. Never put anything away wet (laundry, camping gear, etc.).
2. Well-lit areas don't agree with mildew. Light prevents its growth and can even kill it.
3. Proper ventilation helps prevent mildew spore growth.
4. Cleaning all mildew-prone areas with a disinfectant solution will slow down or stop growth.
5. Put packets of silica gel in small, enclosed, chronically mildewed places (drawers, shoes). The gel can absorb moisture and minimize mildew growth. Reusable bags of calcium chloride (such as Damp Gone) are available for larger areas such as damp rooms or basements. Be sure that no children or pets have access to these packets.

Cigarette Mess

One of the most effective preventive measures you can take is to eliminate smoking from your home. All of us pay a small fortune for the smoking habit—it costs taxpayers millions of dollars daily. Smoking also causes a high percentage of fatal and damaging fires, and can make many jobs unsafe.

Smoke dirties the windows, yellows the light fixtures (so you don't get all the light you pay for), soils and ruins the acoustical tile of the ceiling, stinks up the upholstery, and burns and damages the carpet and floor. Who would consider taking out a miniature incinerator and burning paper, leaves, and trash whenever they got the urge? But that's what a smoker does.

In trying to correct the problem, we designate special smoking areas, make better filters, bigger ashtrays, better vents and room deodorizers. But this is like building a bigger drawer, closet, or garage when the others get full: The problem is still doing damage—it's just contained.

The simplest, cheapest, most effective approach is to dejunk the habit (or at least declare the house a no smoking zone); then the problem will be cut off at the source.

Keep Up

Finally, remember: Dirt by the inch is a cinch; by the yard, it's hard.

Don't get buried alive—clean as you go. Who wants to finish an overhaul, a paint job, or any project and have to clean the entire mess at the end? Clean and put everything back as soon as you finish using it. Don't let it all pile up for a big cleaning spree.

Design Away Cleaning

Cleaning faster and better isn't the only way to reduce the time and expense of cleaning and maintaining a home. How about designing it away?

You've thought this, and you've said it, too. We've all been working on something and stopped to say, "Who designed this? It's twice as hard to clean or fix this way. If it had been better/simpler I could have serviced it in minutes instead of the hours it's taking now." The people who actually do most of the cleaning have thought of many design ideas that would eliminate or ease some hard cleaning chores. But people who do little cleaning have done most of the building. So for centuries the same hard-to-clean, -reach, -lift, and -move things have been built into our homes. Maintenance-freeing design has long been needed, but is only now coming into its own. We'd all like to make things easier to care for, and the logical place to start is the place we spend so much time: our home.

"But my house is already built, so I can't have a maintenance-free home!" *Wrong!* About three-quarters of the possible time-saving changes you can make are in what we professionals call "rollover" items—paint, carpeting, furniture, drapes, fixtures, appliances, and decorations. In five to ten years these often need replacing anyway, so why not do it with something much easier to clean? It's a sneaky, brilliant, fun way to solve cleaning problems and get rid of the time (and agony) they take.

The more I heard people say, "Why do they build things like_____?" the more intrigued I was by the subject of designing to reduce cleaning. So I asked my audiences to share their thoughts on this, and all kinds of bright ideas came rolling in on the best way of all to save cleaning time: Design It Away!

When my collection of material on this subject grew to three-box size and my daughter was working her way through school designing kitchens, we realized there was enough there for a book. After several more years of research and investigation, we assembled all of this material into a nice volume called *Make Your House Do the Housework,* which

Book-of-the-Month Club members and tens of thousands of other people have used to inspire them in their remodeling, redecorating, and new home building. In *Make Your House Do the Housework,* there are hundreds of good ideas for cutting   cleaning  through low-maintenance design. You'll learn about the wisdom of approaches like camouflage, built-in and wall-hung furnishings, better arrangement, artful elimination, and choosing the smart surface, material, and color. The thrill and beauty of it all is that when you change even one single thing to reduce its maintenance requirements, those savings in time and effort are repeated day after day, multiplying even one little improvement into thousands of hours (and a lot of cleaning supplies) saved, and a lot of safety risks avoided, too.

Start thinking about it seriously and your blood will boil with anticipation. Design is one sure way to cut cleaning out of your life!

Check Before You Clean It

Fix those items that always slow you down and cause you to do everything more than once (or actually add to your cleaning chores). Some things aren't worth doing. Some can't be cleaned. Others will look tacky even when they're clean and orderly. Taking care of these items first will not only make cleaning and maintenance easier, but will also make you feel better (which makes everything easier). Eliminate or remove anything that bugs you—anything that's inconvenient, no longer functional, or that you just don't like. Remember: The first principle of efficient cleaning is not to have to do it in the first place. Check these things before you start:

- ☐ Be sure you have plenty of convenient, roomy trash receptacles. You'll do less cleaning and picking up.

- ☐ Be sure you have enough towel racks.

- ☐ Be sure all closets have an adequate supply of hangers.

- ☐ Eliminate furniture you don't use or need. It has no value and multiplies your cleaning chores.

- ☐ Eliminate excess playthings (child or adult)—unused tennis racquets, snowmobiles, motorbikes, games that have fallen from favor, old hobby supplies, puzzles with "only a few pieces missing."

- ☐ Get anything that can be wall-mounted off the floor. It'll make cleaning a lot easier and will curb accumulation. (And eye-level things are easier to see and safer to use.)

☐ See that your cooking exhaust is vented.

☐ Stop all dirt and air leakage into the house around windows and doors, etc. Cracks in the foundation, too, let dust and moisture into the house, causing damage and additional cleaning time.

☐ Make sure your vacuum works perfectly.

☐ Seal all concrete floors for easy maintenance.

☐ Seal any other unfinished surfaces. Paint, varnish, or panel them so they can easily be maintained.

☐ Alter any surface or appearance you don't like. Sand it and paint it, cover it, or replace it.

☐ See that drawer hardware is tight and that drawers slide easily.

☐ Make sure that all doors close tightly and easily. A light sanding and two coats of polyurethane or varnish will make wooden doors bright and easily cleanable, and door tops smooth and easily dusted.

☐ Be sure that all windows slide and lock easily–and seal any cracks.

☐ Repair every leaky or dripping fixture.

☐ Fix or tighten all door handles, stair railings, etc. Check all the hardware around the house. Remember, a 50 cent screw or bolt can save a $5 hinge . . . a $50 door and prevent . . . a $500 robbery . . . a $5,000 fire!

☐ Replace burned-out light bulbs and tighten any parts of light fixtures that need tightening.

☐ Get rid of shin and head bumpers (such as sharp edges or protruding legs) on woodwork, furniture, or anything that bashes you every time you pass by or stand up.

☐ Adjust every shelf to the height you really want and need.

Chapter Nine

Don't Be Caught Streaking Windows

At my housecleaning seminars I always ask the audience, "How many of you like to clean windows?" This is always good for a chorus of groans from everyone present. Occasionally, one or two will wave an eager hand indicating that they, indeed, do enjoy cleaning windows. (Further investigation reveals why: Both have someone else do the job!) That leaves almost 100 percent of home cleaners who hate window cleaning.

The reason is simple. After hours of laboriously polishing windows, you think, "At last. I'm finished!" But hope is dashed when the sun comes up or changes angle. Streaks and smears suddenly appear out of nowhere, magnified for all to see. You again give the window the old college try—and the smears and streaks only change places. Rearming yourself with more window cleaner, rags, and gritty determination, you work even harder and faster to get the windows clean, but they seem only to get worse.

Night falls, and so does the curtain, on a crestfallen and discouraged worker. The next morning you go downtown and eye the fifty-story solid-glass buildings, the huge storefront display windows, and mumble, "That glass is beautiful . . . but I rarely see anyone cleaning it. How do they keep it so clean?"

The reason we seldom see window cleaners isn't because those windows don't need to be done—in fact, many commercial windows have to be cleaned more often than house windows. But professional window cleaners take only minutes—not hours—to do their job. We can be just as effective at home on our own windows if we learn the basic techniques used by the pros.

Many of the concoctions home cleaners try to clean windows with not only create an impossible cleaning situation, but they also prime the glass surface to hold dust, bug spots, and airborne particles. The result is windows that have to be cleaned more often. Even the chief window washers for high-rise glass skyscrapers couldn't get windows streak-free if they used the stuff most of us have under the sink.

The Right Way

To recover all those lost polishing hours, let's learn to clean windows professionally. Go down to the janitorial-supply store and buy a professional-quality brass or stainless steel squeegee (see the equipment chart in Chapter 5). Ettore brand is my favorite. Don't go to the local supermarket or discount house and buy those recycled-truck-tire war clubs they call squeegees. These won't work well even in a professional's hands.

There are even tilt squeegees available that are only slightly more expensive than a standard squeegee. They have a handle that enables you to tilt the blade so you can clean windows from different angles; you don't have to stand directly in front of each window to clean it. A person can stand on the front porch with one and clean all of the upper and lower story windows without changing locations!

You want some window cleaner now, either ammonia or ordinary liquid dish detergent. Both will work well if you use them sparingly; resist the tendency to add too much chemical or detergent to the solution—this causes streaks and leaves residue. One capful of ammonia or four or five drops of dish detergent is plenty in a bucket of warm water.

Keep Your Eye on the Blade

If your squeegee blade gets damaged and starts leaving a line of solution on your windows, pull it out of the channel, turn it over, and snap it back in. When the blade finally wears out, just buy a new blade and slide it into the squeegee channel. (Be sure 1/8 inch of the blade extends beyond each end of the channel.)

When window casings and trim get older, paint and putty chips catch under the squeegee blade and make cleaning miserable. New aluminum or well-maintained wood won't give you any grief. Taking the time to sand and repaint or reglaze will save you many cleaning hours.

Before starting to squeegee, take a damp cloth and run it around the entire outside edge of the window. This removes the cobwebs and debris that collect around windows, so they won't end up on the window itself during cleaning.

Six Steps to Sparkling Windows

1. Put a capful of ammonia or a few drops of dish detergent in a bucket of warm water. There is always a tendency to add too much soap or

detergent—this is what causes streaks and leaves residue.

2. Wet the window lightly with the solution, using a clean sponge, soft-bristle brush, or window-washing wand. You don't need to flood it. If the window is really dirty, go over the moistened area again. Don't push water all the way to the top; it catches underneath and drips later.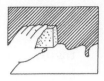

3. Wipe the dry rubber blade of your squeegee with a damp cloth or chamois. A dry blade on any dry glass surface will "peep-a-peep" along and skip places.

4. Next, tilt the squeegee at an angle to the glass so that only about an inch of the rubber blade presses lightly against the top of the window glass (not the window frame or the house shingles). Then pull the squeegee across the window horizontally. This will leave about a one-inch dry strip across the top of the window.

5. Remember all those drips that came running down from the top of your clean window when you tried squeegeeing once before? Well, by squeegeeing across the top first, you've removed that potential stream. Place the squeegee horizontally in the dry area and pull down, lapping over into the dry, clean area each time to prevent any water from running into it. Wipe the blade with a damp cloth or chamois after each stroke. Finish with a horizontal stroke across the bottom to remove the water puddled there.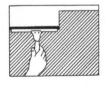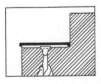

6. Wipe off the bottom of the windowsill with your damp cloth when you're finished.

A window can be cleaned from either side as well as from the top using this same basic technique. Always be sure first to squeegee off that first inch of the glass to eliminate potential dripping. Don't wash windows in direct sunlight if you can possibly avoid it. The solution will dry too fast and streak the glass. If you have to clean in bright sunlight, be extra sure not to put too much cleaner in the water, use cold water, and squeegee *fast!*

How to Get Rid of those Last Spots

After completing a window, you undoubtedly will detect a tiny drop or squeegee mark or two and a little moisture on the edges of the glass near the frame. Your old tendency was to snatch a dry cloth and with a fingertip under it wipe off the edge. This will most likely leave a finger-wide mark right down that edge. Once you notice that, the temptation will be to wipe it again, this time with a bundled cloth. Then you'll have a four-inch mark and will have to reclean the whole window.

After squeegeeing the window, just leave those little beads of side moisture. They'll disappear and you'll never see them. Resist the impulse to use a cloth or paper towel to wipe the last few middle-of-the-window drops. Your bare, oil-free hand, a clean microfiber cloth, or a chamois will do much better. (If you insist, you can catch any remaining drips with a dry microfiber cloth.)

The squeegee method really is as easy as it sounds and it's much faster than the old way. It will use only a penny or two worth of cleaner and leave your windows pure and clean to repel particles and dirt.

It's worth the effort to work on your squeegee technique for a while, since it will be awkward at first. And all of that accumulated gunk might take a little extra effort to remove. Once you catch on, you'll love it and wish you had more windows to do.

Learning to clean windows quickly and effectively will change your outlook on life. You'll cherish the cute little handprints, enjoy watching frustrated insects slip off the glass, and even tolerate the sweet birdies that occasionally befoul your windows.

Problem Areas

Squeegees will work on any normal household window (but not on textured or stained glass, for instance), and they come in sizes to fit the task at hand. Squeegees can also be cut with a hacksaw to custom-fit small panes if you so desire. Pull the rubber blade out of the channel before cutting, and then cut the rubber about ¼ inch longer than the remodeled blade (so it will extend ⅛ inch at each end).

Close Quarters Cleaning

There are times and places in small, confined areas where a spray bottle of fast-evaporating glass cleaner is more efficient to use (on small panes, for handprints on glass entrance doors, on decorative glass in doors, etc.). You can obtain an inexpensive solution of this type in concentrated form from a janitorial-supply store, dilute it with water, spray it lightly on soiled glass, and then buff it dry with a microfiber or clean cotton cloth. Paper towels (the soft, expensive ones) and regular cloths leave lint like crazy. Don't even think about using newspaper.

As for tiny little windows, you can let them go for quite a while, because the visual distraction of all of the intersecting woodwork here has a way of hiding marks, specks, and smudges. When they do need cleaning, depending on their size and how dirty they are, use either a small squeegee or spray and wipe with glass cleaner. Flyspecks and the like may need to be scrubbed a bit with a white nylon scrub sponge.

If the frames are dirty, be sure to wipe or dust them off well before you start on the glass.

If you're not too particular, just brush off the outside, hose them down to rinse them, and call it good. No window in a home is worth hours of work. Big windows show dirt and streaks more readily than small panes, which may even look more "romantic" when they're a bit hazy.

Mirrors

Once people get enthused about a squeegee, they want to use it on everything, even mirrors. Don't! Notice some mirrors have black edges. This means too much cleaning solution was used and it dripped, leached, or otherwise worked its way to the edge of the mirror. When the cleaning solution hit the silver on the back, the chemicals oxidized it. In fact, you shouldn't even spray a mirror (or TV or computer face) with a spray bottle because of possible renegade moisture. Instead, spray into a soft cloth (microfiber, if you have it) and then wipe. **For mirrors, too, a glass cleaner is best.** It's fast, inexpensive, and safe as long as you keep it off the edges.

For no-smudge mirrors, use full-length down-strokes when you wipe. Then with a final swipe across the bottom, eliminate that start-and-stop line.

Plexiglas and Thermal Windows

Plexiglas should have been called plexiplastic, because it doesn't clean like glass at all. Solvents can eat right through it, and anything slightly abrasive (including ordinary dust) will scratch, cloud, and mar it. So "soft" is the word—soft cleaner, soft cloth, soft touch. There are special Plexiglas cleaning solutions that help clean and clear it—don't use anything else!

Don't attempt to wipe or squeegee Plexiglas before you rinse it well with water to remove any particles; otherwise, particles can catch underneath your cleaning cloth or squeegee blade and scratch the surface. And if you squeegee, keep your blade extra clean and make sure the window *stays* wet the whole time you work on it.

Many of the thermal or double-pane windows will fog up when cold, so if the streaks don't come out, check: They're probably on the inside. You can't clean them; most of the time if you want this kind of streak gone it means a new window!

Cleaning Outside Windows

As a precleaning precaution, look at the window carefully before whipping out your fine cleaning tools. Often the window, frame, and sill are plastered with bird droppings, mud, hornet nests, and spider webs complete with dried flies. If so, give the area a quick hose-down first to flush it off. It only takes a minute and makes the final cleaning neater and safer for your squeegee blade.

For dead bugs and other debris lying in the bottom of a sliding window channel, spray generously with all-purpose cleaner and let it sit for five minutes, until it all turns soft. Then wrap a cleaning cloth around a screwdriver blade, insert it in the track, and run it up and down to dislodge and absorb the dirt. Repeat until the channel is clean. It sounds primitive, but it's the fastest and best method.

If you have to clean glass outside on a below-freezing day, mix your cleaning solution 50/50 with some "antifreeze"—isopropyl or denatured alcohol.

High Windows

When windows are out of reach for easy hand or ladder squeegee work, a pole or extension handle of any length you can maneuver will work on the same principle surprisingly well. Clean glass always looks good. A few tiny smudges or

drips won't hurt anything, so don't try to be a perfectionist. It isn't worth the stress or time. I use an Ettore extension handle that extends from 4 to 8 feet. Even second-story windows are quick to do, and your feet never leave the ground. You don't need a ladder and there's no safety risk.

When you use an extension pole, instead of wiping the squeegee after each stroke, just hit the pole with the palm of your hand to release excess water from the blade.

Second-story windows can be done easily with a squeegee on an extension handle and your feet never leave the ground. No ladder is needed and there's no safety risk.

Hard-Water Deposits

If you have hard-water buildup on outside windows from sprinklers, don't use abrasive cleanser or the glass will cloud and scratch. If the deposit isn't too thick and hasn't been on there too long, Showers-n-Stuff (see the equipment chart in Chapter 5) or a mild acid cleaner will remove the deposit. Spray on the solution, let it work a minute, and then scrub it with a white nylon scrub sponge until it dissolves. Rinse and repeat if needed. If you have a real accumulation welded on, it'll take several applications, with the cleaner left on for a longer time. Don't lose patience if it doesn't wipe right off.

For the toughest hard-water haze, there is a very strong commercial-grade paste that must be used with caution. It's called Once-Over. Write to me at PO Box 700, Pocatello, ID 83204 for information about ordering it, or send an e-mail to Customer Support at *www.cleanreport.com*.

After all this, if it's still white and opaque, your window may be etched and damaged. Replace the glass or draw the drapes. Keep hard water off your windows with regular maintenance or an adjustment in your sprinkling system.

Window Scraping Woes

A lot of window damage is done when paint, labels, or mortar are being removed from windows. Here's the right way to go about cleanup operations on glass:

1. Before you start scraping a window with anything, try to soak off the foreign material with plain water. Then try a solvent such as De-Solv-it.
2. Always keep the glass surface wet when scraping.
3. Use only razor-sharp blades or flat razor-type tools in a one-way forward motion, then lift the tool off the glass and make another forward stroke. Never go back and forth. Pulling the tool back and forth will eventually trap a piece of grit or sand behind and under the blade, which will scratch even a wet window.
4. Don't use abrasive scrub pads or compounds on window glass.
5. Be careful. Too much pressure, or an abrupt or careless motion, could get you a nasty cut as well as a broken pane.

Cleaning Window Accessories

Though windows themselves are not hard to clean, there is usually a lot more than just glass to clean here. Cleaning and dusting window accessories is not strictly a cinch, because windows attract bugs, pets, people, and moisture from condensation. Fortunately, just as professional window-washing methods can have glass looking its best with minimum effort on your part, a little attention to technique can keep your screens, blinds, and curtains looking sharp.

Screens

When your screens become embedded with dead bugs, tree sap, dirt, bird droppings, and other unsightly debris, take them down. Spread out an old rug or quilt or piece of canvas on the ground outside, and lay your screens *flat* (this is important to avoid damage) on it. Mix up some all-purpose cleaner solution and scrub the screens with a soft-bristled brush. Rinse the screens with a hose, give them a sharp rap with your hand to jar most of the water loose, and let them finish drying in the sun.

Shades

If window shades are going to come clean, a dry sponge (see page 51) will do it. The sturdier plastic or plastic-coated shades can be damp-wiped with all-purpose cleaner. Remember that shades get sun-rotted and discolored over time, so don't be disappointed if they don't look picture-perfect when you're finished.

Blinds

Whether they are the old Venetian type or the newer minis, blinds are such a pain to clean that some home cleaners have cheerfully given up the privacy and easy light adjustment that blinds undeniably provide. If you haven't yet reached that point, you might never have to if you clean blinds this way.

The big secret of blind maintenance isn't any "magic fingers" you send away for. It's simply dusting often enough so that the dust doesn't have a chance to blend with airborne oils into that stubborn, grimy coating we all know and hate. This means at least a monthly run over the blinds with a lambswool duster (see the equipment chart in Chapter 5), making firm contact with the surface. Close the blinds before you start, and when you've done one side, close them in the other direction and do the other side.

Vertical blinds don't collect dust and airborne soils as swiftly as the horizontals. But they should be dusted frequently too (at least every few months might be enough here), for the same reason.

Sooner or later blinds will need to be washed. Don't try to do this without taking them down; washing blinds in place is slow and messy, and you'll curse yourself for attempting it. Don't wash them in the sink or bathtub either. Take them outside. If you can, find a slanting surface, such as a driveway; if not, a flat surface will do. Lay down an old quilt, blanket, or canvas drop cloth first, and then lay the blinds on it to prevent them from being damaged.

Let out each blind to full length and close it, making sure the louvers are flat. Lay the blind on the cushioning cloth and scrub with the direction of the slats, using a soft-bristled brush and all-purpose cleaner. Then reverse the blind and wash the other side. The cloth will get soapy and help clean the blind.

Hang or hold up the blind and rinse it with a hose (a helper is very useful at this point). Shake off the excess water and let the blind dry thoroughly before rehanging it.

Cloth-covered verticals should be cleaned more often because their soft surface will absorb dirt, which can be baked on by the sun. Don't use a lambswool duster or treated dust cloth of any kind on cloth-covered blinds—again because of their absorbency. Vacuum them with a dust brush attachment instead. Clean cloth-covered verticals a couple of times a year by taking a cloth dampened with carpet shampoo solution and lightly wiping the surface.

The most painless way to clean blinds is to send them out to a professional for ultrasonic cleaning. (Just look in your local phone book under Blinds—Cleaning.) This gets the slats, ladders, cords—*everything*—sparkling clean.

Drapes

Buy good-quality drapes, and check regularly to make sure they stay hung properly. Vacuum drape tops and sides occasionally. When you clean the floor near full-length drapes, protect them by slipping the bottom of the panel through an ordinary clothes hanger and hooking the top over the rod.

You can refurbish drapes not dirty enough to be cleaned by running them through the clothes dryer on a cool setting. (*Don't* do this with fiberglass drapes; they'll leave an irritating residue in the dryer that will transfer itself to clothing.) Be sure to remove any drapery hooks first.

Since drapes are relatively inexpensive to dry-clean, get estimates from a couple of different shops. **Having them cleaned professionally is often less of a hassle than doing them yourself.**

Check your drapes by slapping them in the sunshine. If they've been collecting dirt, you'll see it. If they're faded and threadbare and the dirt is all that's holding them together, it's time to go shopping.

A simple coat hanger will protect drapes from damage during carpet cleaning.

Chapter Ten

Floors Under Your Foot and Rule

The floor, more than any other part of the house, projects the overall image of your home. The chances of anyone noticing that all-day sucker stuck to the patio door, the half-eaten wiener on the bookcase, or the cobweb across Grandpa's picture are lessened if the floors are clean and brilliant.

The term "hard floors" didn't originate as a description of the effort needed to clean them; it's simply used to distinguish them from carpeted, or soft, floors. Hard floors include vinyl, linoleum, wood, ceramic and other tiles, terrazzo, stone, cork, dirt (nothing under it), and good old concrete. All hard floors have their purpose, they all get harder use than just about any other part of the house, and they all have to be cleaned and maintained. Doing that cleaning and maintenance the professional way will give you the results you want with far less time and effort.

Another reminder here before we start: Floors require much less cleaning if you provide good entrance matting (see Chapter 8). Hundreds of hours of floor problems and worries will disappear if you install professional-quality mats at all entrances to stop dirt and abrasives from getting into your house. Some wear and damage to hard floors comes with time, foot traffic, and exposure to sunlight. But most wear, discoloration, and deterioration of flooring materials and any finish on them come from dirt and grit abrading the surface of the floor. Keeping the surface clean will greatly prolong the life of a floor and any finish on it.

Are hard or soft floors easier to keep clean? It depends. In high-traffic or high-abuse areas, hard flooring is better. In low-traffic, low-abuse areas, carpeting is easier and faster to care for. Overall, hard floors are more sanitary than carpeting because they can be cleaned more easily and thoroughly.

How to Clean Hard Floors

The most important way to keep floors looking good indefinitely is simple: Keep them clean! That doesn't just mean removing roller skates, cat toys, coins, combs and clothes, either. It's the dust, grit, gravel, sand, food crumbs, and other such substances that remain on floors, abrade them, and eventually get ground into powder and embed themselves in the surface that cause your cleaning woes. Once all this "dirt power" is on the loose, it will destroy a floor rapidly. Keep hard floors well swept (even when you can't see dirt and dust).

You can, of course, vacuum a hard-surface floor, and it does get all the dust and crumbs from corners and hard-to-reach crevices. On smaller hard-surface floors, especially parts of hard flooring right next to other vacuum jobs, it's smart maneuvering to just hit them with the vacuum while you're at it (and it saves stooping with a dustpan). Most vacuums today do a good job on hard-surface floors, or have attachments that will. Uprights, like the Windsor, or a canister or backpack vacuum with a floor brush attachment are great for hardwood, vinyl, tile, and concrete. Don't use a vacuum with a beater bar on a hard floor, especially wood—even if the beater doesn't dent the floor it can, at its rapid rotation rate, fling grit or gravel into the floor and chip the surface.

On very large hard floors, vacuuming is slow, noisy, and inefficient; use a professional 14- or 18-inch treated dust mop. It's faster, more effective, and will last much longer than anything you can pick up at the supermarket. Brooms stir up dust all over the place and leave fine unseen particles that will be ground into your wax and eventually destroy the finish. **A good dust mop is much faster and does a much better job than a broom.** There's no comparison, especially if you have a good-quality pro dust mop with a full-circle swivel head. A dust mop will cover a lot of ground quickly and is flat enough to get under furniture. It will gather gravel, paper clips, gum wrappers, safety pins, and the 100 other items that find their way to the floor. It will also pick up and hold the dust. A dust mop, especially a treated dust mop, is unbelievably effective on sealed concrete basement and garage floors. Treat your dust mop by spraying the head with a little Endust, furniture polish, or professional dust mop treatment. You can also take the head off the frame and pour a couple of tablespoons of furniture polish into the pocket; let it set at least twelve hours before mopping. Don't overtreat mops or they can make the floor slippery.

Before you start, use a counter brush or angle broom to detail the edges of the floor so you don't accumulate a buildup in the corners. If you use a broom to do this, run it along the tops of the baseboards too, and use the angled point to clean out corners.

When you mop, use S strokes and keep the mop in contact with the floor, but don't bear down on it—pressure isn't necessary. The mop will turn and swivel under furniture (one of the advantages of a professional-quality mop). Always lead with the same edge and don't lift the head from the floor until you've finished or you'll lose your dust load. Mop next to the baseboard last.

If you have only a small amount of hard flooring, do it by hand with a cleaning cloth (see pages 204-205 for details on how to make and use a cleaning cloth), Scrubbee Doo dust mop head, or dust cloth. You won't need a commercial dust mop.

When you need to sweep, the corn broom has been around a long time and can serve well if you remember it's only for dry work. If you do sweep anything wet, don't set the broom on the straw end afterward to dry or it'll develop a permanent curl.

The best broom out there is the nylon angle head type. The bristles have fine split tips to get up even the most minute stuff, and lots of springy strength to pull the rocks and toys along, should you need to sweep that hard. The angled head reaches into corners better, and it better suits our natural sweeping stroke. These plastic brooms shed less and last longer (which is easier on the pocketbook and our dumpsites)—water, snow, chemicals, or chasing the chickens won't hurt them.

For outdoor or rough-surfaced expanses of hard flooring, a push broom is what you want—with an eighteen- or twenty-four-inch nylon bristle head and good, sturdy handle braces.

To pick up the final whisk of dirt that the dustpan and broom won't get, grab a piece of paper out of the garbage, or from an old newspaper or magazine, and wet it. Wipe the area with it, and those tiny particles all stick to the wet paper. Not a speck will be left on the floor.

Damp-Mopping

The most important operation (after vacuuming, dust-mopping, or sweeping to remove loose dirt and debris) is damp-mopping, which is done to remove the film of dirt, settled airborne grease, and sticky spills that accumulate from daily use.

The equipment needed to wet-clean your floors depends on the amount and type of hard-surfaced floors you have.

Some homes have so much wall-to-wall carpet that only the kitchen and bathroom have hard floors.

If a hard floor is in the center of the house where considerable travel over carpeted areas is required to reach it, any wax or finish on it (see page 127) will last for months if the floor is kept clean. You could clean the floor by hand in about fifteen minutes a year. A sponge mop (see the equipment chart in Chapter 5 for the superior professional model of these) is adequate damp-mopping equipment in 80 percent of modern homes.

If you have several rooms of vinyl, tile, or wood floors, as well as a big game room, garage, and patio or storage area, some basic labor-saving floor tools would be a good investment (again, see the equipment chart in Chapter 5). Get a good twelve- or sixteen-ounce string mop, preferably a rayon/cotton Layflat, and a good mop bucket. Wheels on a household mop bucket aren't necessarily what you want, since we rarely move the bucket when we just mop the kitchen floor; besides, wheels make a bucket heavier and more awkward. But you do want *something* to squeeze the moisture out of your mops so you don't have to tromp on them with your foot or do it with your bare hands. Wringing mops by hand is finger suicide: The things your mop picks up—pins, glass, etc.—will lacerate your hands. The built-in roller wringer types are good, and so are the small versions of the commercial handle-squeezer type. The price of a small commercial mop bucket might shock you, but it will be a time-saver and will greatly contribute to the quality of work you can do.

How to Damp-Mop

Dipping a mop in a bucket of plain or soapy water and swabbing the place down is not mopping. It gives the floor a temporary wet look, but when it dries it won't look much better than it did to begin with. Magnificent moppers remember these basics:

1. *Use the right solution.* Mopping with plain or vinegar water (unless you have laminate flooring) is an exercise in futility, and it's wasted wear and tear on a good mop. Without a surfactant (chemical that helps the solution to penetrate) and emulsifier (to help break up and dissolve the dirt), moisture alone does little to a floor or to the soil on it. On the other hand, too strong a solution will degloss the floor and cause filming or streaks. So use just a bit of neutral all-purpose cleaner (one ounce per gallon of warm water). You want to cut the dirt but not the wax or the finish. Mix up your mopping solution in a plain bucket and have your wringer bucket handy.

2. *Always sweep or dust-mop the floor thoroughly before you start.* Even better, vacuum it. This is one time the thoroughness of vacuuming is a real advantage. If you don't get up all the loose dirt and debris first, you're just going to soil the floor further by mopping it.

3. *"Frame" the floor first.* Run the mop around the edges of the floor, to a point 10 to 12 inches from the baseboard. Then when you mop the middle (see the next step), stay 10 to 12 inches away from the wall. This eliminates the buildup that mopping can deposit along the baseboard. Slapping the mop on the baseboard will result in a filthy edge.

4. *Mop all the rest in a "figure 8" from side to side out in front of you.* Mopping like this is less fatiguing because you use the big muscles of your midbody and hips, rather than your wrists and arms; it also covers more ground in less time. You also overlap more, so there are fewer missed spots.

5. *Keep your mop clean.* Always wring the dirty water into your wringer bucket before you dip the mop back into the bucket full of cleaning solution.

6. *Flop your mop!* Turn the mop head over often. Water is heavy, so when you pick up water with a mop it will always accumulate at the bottom of the mop as you work

with it. This is why you need to flip the mop over every two or three strokes, to get a drier side. When you use a mop to apply solution or "scrub," you flop it to get to a cleaner side. When you've flopped the mop several times and it won't pick up any more water or it's completely dirty, wring it out.

7. *Go over the floor twice.* Make two passes over the same surface: the first to wet and dissolve, the second to remove. So first spread the solution out over the floor (but don't flood it), and let it sit on there a minute (or a little longer if the floor is extra dirty) so the cleaner can attack and emulsify the dirt. Then wring the mop dry and go over the whole area again, removing all the moisture and dirt possible. If you've mixed up the solution right—not too much cleaner—and mopped the floor good and dry on the second pass, you'll be done. If you put on too much solution and leave it on too long, it'll cut the wax. And if you don't make a second pass to remove your cleaning solution, there'll be lots of detergent residue when the water evaporates, leaving the floor sticky and cloudy.

Mop Miscellaneous

- *The telltale four:* If you find more than four mop strings in the bottom of the bucket after cleaning the floor, it's time to get a new mop head. With all the time they spend wet, they do disintegrate after a while.

- *Why do you want a rayon/cotton rather than all-cotton mop?* Because the strands will be stronger, so there will be fewer of them left behind on the chair legs and in corners.

- *Damp-mopping means what it says.* Wring out all the possible moisture before putting mop to floor. Excess water runs into cracks and corners and down to the subfloor, and it won't do any good in any of these places. Over time, the subfloor can be damaged.

- *Keep a couple of nylon scrub sponges (one backed with white nylon, one with green) handy when you mop, so you can make quick work of stubborn "glued-on" spots, spills, and scuffs.* If a dampened white sponge doesn't work, move up to the green one. A plastic scraper is also handy here.

- *Watch the handle when you raise a mop to put it in the wringer.* Pro cleaners know only too well that if you're not careful you can wreck ceiling tile or break light fixtures and be injured by falling glass.

Wax It!

Most hard floors need a protective coating to keep them looking good longer. Floors will wear out much faster if they're not protected. Floors claiming to be "no-wax" will also dull in traffic areas if not protected by a finish of some kind. The "never need to wax" claims for vinyl flooring, for instance, just don't hold up. If you expect such a floor to stay shiny in heavy traffic areas, it needs a dressing. Laminate floors are the exception.

There are four good reasons for you to apply floor finish or "wax" to most hard floors:

1. *Appearance:* A beautiful floor is an exhilarating experience for the beholder and a reward for the home cleaner. A coat of wax fills in the tiny scratches and worn spots on a floor to make it look like new again.

2. *Protection:* Even the hardest surfaces will scuff, wear, and dull with grinding foot traffic, spills, and chemical cleaners. A wax or other protective finish covering the surface lessens abrasion and other damage and lengthens the life of most hard floors. Even "no-wax" floors need

a dressing or finish to prevent the surface from being dulled and damaged over time.

3. *Cleanability:* Soil, dirt, spills, marks of all kinds, and abrasive residues are much simpler to clean from a smooth, well-waxed or finished surface. Sweeping a well-used unwaxed or unfinished tile floor will take you 25 percent longer than sweeping a highly polished one. A coat of wax or other finish on the floor is like a coat of varnish on a bare wood table: It seals the surface and keeps soils and oils from penetrating it. Wiping something from the top of a protective nonpenetrable finish takes only seconds. It sure beats spending hours trying to scrub it out once it has soaked in and stained.

4. *Safety:* Contrary to what most people think, shiny, well-waxed, and properly maintained floors are generally less slippery than bare floors. Bare, porous, worn floors have a slick, flint-hard surface whether wet or dry. A coat or two of wax or acrylic finish actually cushions the floor. This could be compared to laying a thin cloth or cover over a bare plastic tabletop; it creates a surface that won't let things slide around. Thus a coat or "cover" of wax makes most floors less slippery.

How to Wax a Floor

If a floor has been waxed previously (or many times previously), and the old wax is dirty and grimy looking, it is time to strip it off and rewax. Fortunately today's floor finishes are "nonyellowing," so they stay looking good much longer and extend the time before it is necessary to strip the floor.

If old wax or finish is due to come off, you can make that hard job an easy one. Sweep the floor first and then round up two buckets: an ordinary bucket and a mop bucket. Fill the mop bucket three-quarters full with clean water—don't put cleaner in it. Mix some warm water and wax stripper in the ordinary bucket. A detergent cleaner will do fine for a light scrub, but if you want all the wax off, use a commercial wax remover. Ammonia cuts wax, but it can also cut the plasticizers in the floor if you leave it on too long! A nonammoniated commercial wax remover will do the best and safest job.

Dip your fresh mop into the solution and apply it to the floor generously so that the solution can attack the old wax and dirt. Cover as large an area as you feel you can clean and wipe up before it dries. (This area will probably be about 10 feet by 10 feet.) Remember, use the basic principle of cleaning explained in Chapter 6: As soon as the solution is on the floor, old wax and dirt begin to be dissolved and suspended and can soon be wiped off easily.

This may be a bit optimistic, because chances are that you have some spots where wax buildup is as thick as cardboard and as hard as concrete. It will need scrubbing or scraping, and possibly another application or two of solution. If so, scrub with a hand floor scrubber (see the equipment chart in Chapter 5). It has a long handle with a plastic "gripper" on its end that holds a five-by-ten-inch nylon pad. Edges are especially easy with one of these little gems. One hand scrubber could probably outdo five small household electric scrubbers.

If you use a floor machine, the pro single-disk models are far better than the little units normally made for home use. Keep an eye on the classified section of your paper and you might find a used twelve- or thirteen-inch professional unit for less than $100. Use nylon scrubbing and polishing pads under a floor machine for best results—brushes are almost worthless. For wax removal, the brown or black pads are the best.

When the solution on the floor looks creamy and gunky, it means the dirt and old wax are coming loose. Before you remove the stripper, check the floor with your fingernail. If your nail looks like your kid's, the wax is not fully removed. Use more solution and, if necessary, scrub a little.

This is a good time to resolve not to let the floor get in this condition again!

Most floor-stripping time is spent trying to get wax off unused areas, such as under the end table and TV, and off the edges of the floors. Previously, when you rewaxed the traffic paths or worn areas that needed it, you also gave a generous coat to the edges, the areas beneath furniture, and all the other places that didn't need it. This system of application was repeated year after year. A traffic area will come clean easily because there's no buildup, but the thick areas will need lots of work to get off the buildup. Next time, don't rewax the floors where you don't use them. Once you've given the entire floor one coat of wax and more coats are to be applied, put the additional coats on *traffic areas only*.

There is another way to avoid buildup: When you wax the floor, apply the first one or two coats to the traffic areas and middle of the floor only. Then do the entire floor, including the edges, in your last coat. This will give the floor a uniform appearance without causing buildup on the edges and low-traffic areas.

Now, back to cleaning the floor. The floor is soaked and scrubbed, the wax and dirt are loosened, and it's a mess. Don't pull out that mop and try to sop or slop it up. Instead, reach for a simple, inexpensive tool called a floor squeegee (see the equipment chart in Chapter 5). Or you can use an old window squeegee you have lying around (not your nice new one, which should be used only for windows). Squeegee the gunk into a puddle on the uncleaned area (mind you don't squeegee it down a heating vent), and use an ordinary dustpan to quickly scoop up the gunk and dump it into a bucket. (I once met a woman who used a turkey baster to suck it up, but I'm sticking with the dustpan.) The squeegeed area will be almost perfectly clean, except for a possible drop or two from the squeegee lap.

A squeegee will do a great job on all hard floors—even fairly rough concrete, or vinyl floors with relief designs (the little crud-catching indentations or pits that really are the pits to clean). If the floor has some deep, bad cracks between tiles, you can use a wet-dry vacuum with a squeegee attachment to pull out the liquid.

Now for the mop. . . . Rinse it in clear water and then damp-mop the area. Add a little vinegar to the mop water to neutralize any alkaline residue from the cleaner so the wax will bond better. If the floor was really gunky, rinse again with clean water. Let the floor dry, and the area is ready to wax. Repeat this process until the whole floor is finished. All the gunk will end up in one bucket, to be dumped in the toilet (*not* the sink). The mop water will remain fresh and work for the entire floor because it only rinses the squeegeed floor. (And just think: You never had your hands in filthy water.)

When the floor is dry, apply a first light coat of wax to the entire floor. Put two more thin coats on your traffic paths—don't rewax areas that don't get heavy wear. Use a good professional metal interlock or acrylic finish, obtainable at any janitorial-supply store.

Wax Wisdom

- *Just because it shines doesn't mean it's clean.* Those mop-and-shine products lay a gloss on top of your floor that reflects light. When you're finished, where's the dirt? Under the wax. Likewise, be sure to remove the grimy scrub water before applying any finishing product, or you may just have shiny dirt.

- *Pros wax floors with a clean string mop, but a full-sized (thirty-six-ounce) mop is huge.* The next time one of your small mops gets older or hardened at the ends, trim it to six- or eight-ounce size and wax with it, just as if you were damp-mopping. It's faster than an applicator and it applies wax perfectly. Rinse the mop well with hot water afterward or you'll have a plaster-hard wax mop!

The Right Way to Remove Old Wax

1. Spread solution on the floor in an area you can handle at one time—about 10 by 10 feet. Then let it sit to dissolve old hard wax. If you see that the stripper solution is drying too fast, add more stripper solution from your bucket so the solution on the floor doesn't dry. Dried stripper solution is extremely difficult to remove from a floor.

2. Now scrub with a hand floor scrubber or floor machine with a stripping pad. Go over the area twice.

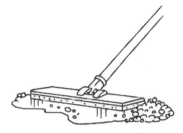

3. Test the floor with a fingernail to see if all the old wax is dissolved.

4. With an old squeegee or a floor squeegee (not your window squeegee), squeegee up the dirty mucky slop water.

6. Now rinse. Use a little vinegar in the water to neutralize the floor. This is important because the stripper is highly alkaline and if the surface isn't neutralized the new wax won't bond to it.

5. Then scoop up the sloppy puddle into a dustpan and dispose of it.

- *Most floor finishes and waxes are delicately balanced chemically.* Mixing them with water or other wax—or even waxing over an unrinsed floor—will cause them to yellow, powder, streak, and perform poorly. Use them pure.
- *Three is better than one:* When applying floor finish or wax, remember that several (two or three) thin coats beat one big heavy coat. It's better for looks, durability, and even drying!

Tile Floors

There must be 400 brands, 500 styles, and at least 1,000 different colors and patterns of clay and masonry floor tiles to choose from. And it's pretty clear from all the calls, letters, e-mails, and questions I get from people concerning "their new tile" that everyone thinks they picked the wrong one. Seldom does any tile give you all you expected, but many tile problems can be cured with a little adjustment in the approach and cleaning product you use, especially by simply coming to understand and accept the properties of the floor tile you have now.

In general, tile has a very hard surface that can take abuse and wear and requires minimal maintenance. The stickler is that tile comes in everything from a slick, glossy surface to a dull, porous one. Your tile could be one of these or one of the many variations in between.

Lots of people who have bought the shiny tile call me and say, "I don't like the shininess. It shows every streak of dirt. What can I do?" Well, that is the tile's nature and personality, the way it was designed—its slick surface reflects light and thus it shines. Shiny surfaces also won't hold finish or "wax"; the finish powders and flakes off because the surface is too slippery to bond to. But that same slick, hard surface won't allow dirt or spills to penetrate and it is easy to clean.

The next most frequent question I get about tile floors is, "I can't make my 'Mexican tile' floor shine!" That's right.

Unglazed clay or quarry tile like this was designed to be rough and porous to provide traction, and it absorbs rather than reflects light. This means it won't shine. If you put enough coats of sealer and finish on, you may see some shine, but it takes a lot of applications and continual maintenance. Again, you can't change the personality of the tile.

A Few More Truths about Tile

- *Remove the residue.* Two of the most common mistakes on shiny tile are mopping in a way that leaves soap residue behind (which kills the luster), or mopping with plain water, vinegar and water, or something that doesn't cut the grease and dirt so the floor stays dull and sticky. You have to mop or scrub a tile floor with a good cleaner (such as neutral all-purpose cleaner), making sure you mix it up exactly as the manufacturer recommends, no stronger— and then make sure you get rid of all the traces of that cleaner when you're done. To accomplish this, rinse-mop with plain water afterward or add a little vinegar to the rinse water (it doesn't clean, but it will neutralize any alkalinity left on the floor). Check this out if your ceramic tile isn't as sparkling as you want it. If you have lots of tile, get a little thirteen-inch single-disk floor polisher from a janitorial-supply store and, with a white nylon pad, buff or "burnish" the tile after it's been cleaned to remove hard-water deposits and other stubborn stains and bring up its natural luster. This will only take a minute or two.
- *Coat it.* If you have one of the more porous types of tile and insist on some shine, you can put a coating (sealer or finish) on it to fill the pores, prevent dirt penetration, and give it a bit of a glow. (You don't ever want to seal or wax ceramic tile, pavers, stone, or brick floors, though.)
- Since I don't know which of the 500 tiles you may have out there in Stamford, Tampa, Albuquerque, or Billings,

I suggest you go down to the local janitorial-supply store and ask what they would recommend for tile of your type or what the local contractors use to enhance floors like yours. Then you'll know what you can use and where to get it. But be sure the floor is properly prepared first—well cleaned, rinsed, and neutralized if necessary, or the finish will quickly flake or powder off. Finish will also fail to adhere over any greasy or oily spots.

- *Seal the grout.* On most tile, the grout is the biggest problem. The mortar between the tiles gets porous (or was that way to begin with), so dirt and stains get in it and when you clean they don't come out. Untreated masonry like this, just like a plain cement garage floor, will absorb everything and quickly get cruddy. Clean and rinse your tile floor well, especially the grout (you may need a degreaser to get out all that embedded oily dirt). Then let it dry well and get some grout sealer (your local tile dealer should have this), and use a small paintbrush to apply the seal to the grout; it will be well worth it. The sealer, usually a silicone, fills the pores of the grout so that it resists dirt and buildup.

- *The secret of intelligent selection.* All of you who were going to get a tile floor, don't panic! I was once very gun-shy on tile, but now I'm putting mostly tile floors in the low-maintenance buildings I'm constructing. The way to make a smart choice is to look around at tile that is already in use. Some tile, especially in shopping malls, always looks beautiful, and with little maintenance. Contact the architect of the place with the tile you admire and find out what it is—"showroom selection" is often maintenance misery.

If you have carpet butting up against ceramic tile flooring, be sure to replace any metal bar in your vacuum beater with another brush. The metal bar (great for bouncing the carpet to loosen soil) can chip your tile if you happen to lap over onto it.

Coping with Concrete Floors

Dust-mopping concrete floors is a trick most of us haven't heard of. Concrete floors, believe it, or not, are almost equal in square footage to carpet in many American homes. Unfinished full basements are common. People often intend to finish them, but they wait many years—"until we can afford to build those two bedrooms and a family room in the basement." Garages, too, usually have concrete flooring, and garages are bigger than ever these days. Both of these areas bear a constant flow of traffic back and forth into the "finished" part of the house. Concrete absorbs and holds stains and marks, and the surface of concrete (which is made of sand, cement, lime and additives) "bleeds" dust and grit, which end up circulating through your house. So concrete is responsible for more cleaning time than you might realize.

Go get your broom right now and sweep your basement or garage. Leave the pile of residue and go back and sweep again just as carefully. The second pile will amaze you, as will the third if you sweep again. Because concrete is textured and porous and "bleeds," vacuuming it is really the only way to get it dustless, and even so, after use it will again be dusty. If you want to eliminate hundreds of hours of direct and indirect adverse results from concrete floors in your home, seal the concrete. You've walked on many a sealed floor in supermarket, malls, stadiums, on ramps, around pools, etc.; they look like they're varnished. Sealed concrete is easy to maintain and will last for years.

You Can Seal Your Own Concrete Floors

Concrete has to cure at least twenty-eight days after pouring before it's ready to seal. It's best to seal concrete floors before they're ever used, because oil stains and other fluids may penetrate and will be difficult or impossible to remove, and the seal will magnify any pre-existing marks. For that matter, seal may be unable to penetrate or adhere to oil stains or other residue that has worked its way into the surface of the concrete.

On either old or new concrete, sweep up all surface dirt and remove everything possible from the floor (furniture, tools, etc.). Mop on a solution of strong alkaline cleaner or, better still, etching acid diluted in water. (Your janitorial-supply store or paint store will have these.) Let it soak in for a while to remove the lime and debris on the surface of the concrete, leaving a firm, clean base. If the floor is old and marked, scrub it with a floor machine, or your trusty hand floor scrubber. Even if you don't scrub, apply the solution and let it sit. Then flush off the solution, using your floor squeegee. Rinse with a hose. Allow the floor to dry well.

You can get penetrating seal at paint or janitorial-supply stores. The latest generation of water-based concrete seals are wonderful! Apply the seal according to directions with any applicator that will distribute it in a thin, even coat; let it dry. Most concrete seals are self-leveling, so it should turn out okay, but a second coat will make sure all the "etched," rough surface areas are filled. Don't try to save the used applicator. It isn't worth cleaning out.

Once the seal is dry, you have a shiny, glossy, smooth (not slick) surface that can be waxed and maintained just like any hard floor. Stains, oil spills, pet indiscretions, etc., can be wiped off without leaving the usual ugly, penetrating mark. Sealed concrete finish wears well. Chips and scrapes can be touched up with a small paintbrush or cloth.

Wood Floors

Homeowners are in awe of their wood floors; literally thousands of them have written or called me with fears and worries about wood. Wood is a warm, handsome surface that will last and look good indefinitely if you treat it right. The old way to maintain wood floors was to apply a penetrating oil and then put a layer of solvent (or "spirit") wax over it. This method does protect the floor to a degree, but it doesn't provide a hard, permanent, waterproof coating. It's also a lot of work, and the floor always looks like a seedy barroom floor needing only a layer of sawdust and a moose head to complete the atmosphere.

The better way to protect your wood is to apply two or three coats of polyurethane-type finish or varnish to a wood floor. Like a thin sheet of glass, this will seal off the wood from moisture, wear, and abuse. Any maintenance you do after that isn't going to touch the wood itself. Water doesn't hurt well-

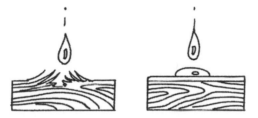

sealed wood if used wisely—which means used sparingly and not left on for long. Be sure the sealer or finish is intact (no cracks or worn spots), because once moisture gets into wood it swells the grain and pops off the finish; it can even discolor and warp the floor.

Once the floor is well sealed, pick up any spills quickly, dust-mop or sweep frequently to keep the floor free of dust and grit, and damp-mop occasionally with a neutral all-purpose-cleaner, getting that water on and off quickly.

Keep wooden floors covered with a protective polyurethane or varnish floor finish. If moisture penetrates wood it will swell and pop off the finish; then the wood deteriorates rapidly.

Even a well-varnished floor will look dull when it's worn and scratched, so that's why I like to wax them. You can use paste wax, but it's slow hands-and-knees stuff—a nice liquid acrylic with a high solids content (such as Top Gloss) will work as well with much less effort. The wax keeps the polyurethane (which is protecting the wood) from getting scratched. But don't try to wax freshly sealed wood, or the finish won't stick. Use the floor for a month or two to reduce the gloss, and the wax will adhere.

Refinishing Wood Floors

Shy away from sanding wood floors except as a last resort. An eighth of an inch of wood taken off a three-quarter-inch floor really affects its performance. Cracks, crowns, and cupping will appear and squeaks will develop.

Sometimes, especially if you're rehabbing a much-abused old house, you'll have no choice but to sand down the floors. But chances are, if your wood floors are old and ugly, the problem's not the wood, but the layers of layered, cracked finish. If you sand it down, the old finish will gum up the belts of the sander, and it will be a mess. Plus, you'll lose part of your floor. Instead, try this: Buy a gallon or two of varnish or paint remover and apply it generously to the floor. The old varnish will instantly crumble and release its hold on the wood. Scrape it well, and then use your trusty floor squeegee and dustpan to pick up the mess. This should leave the floor bare. If some old varnish does remain, use a little more remover and scrape some more—it will come off.

Then go over the entire floor lightly with a screen-back sanding disk. Vacuum the floor well and apply one coat of polyurethane or varnish; thin down this first coat so it will soak into the wood. After it dries, apply one or two more coats, depending on the condition of the floor. Soft or worn wood generally needs two coats to achieve a good gloss.

You won't believe how good your floor will look or how easy the job will be. Just be sure to read all the directions that come with floor care products, and don't be afraid to ask the dealer questions.

To move heavy furniture and appliances easily without scratching the floor—a thick towel slipped under each leg will help the unit slide for easy cleaning access.

Remember Daily Maintenance for Protection

After you've expended all the time and effort to get your floors clean and shiny, keep them clean daily and they'll last for years. Remember, it's the spills, crumbs, sand, dust, etc., that create the conditions that make you work. If a few black marks get on the floor, they'll be on top of the wax, and you can easily remove them with a moist nylon cleaning pad on the end of your hand floor scrubber. The most efficient way to keep hard floors clean is to dust mop them daily.

A Few Final Words about Floors

Remember, good matting at exterior and interior entrances will save you more floor work than all the gimmicks, tips, and miracle floor formulas combined. Avoid "one-stroke" miracle combinations that clean and wax your floor at the same time. When family members are choosing footwear, try to avoid the kind that leaves black marks on a floor.

Some floors are much easier to maintain than others, so don't break your neck trying to make your floor shine like those you see on commercials. Some floor material, because it's cheap, damaged, porous, discolored, or just plain ugly, is almost impossible to make look good. Some floors need three or four coats of wax to build them up to a gloss. A good shine will hide a lot. If a floor won't shine, or is difficult to maintain, consider replacing it or carpeting it.

When you put in new flooring, get the best quality you can afford and stick to tested, reliable surfaces. Remember that solid colors are tougher to maintain and keep looking good. Try to avoid flooring with heavy texturing or indentations. Smooth-surfaced floors are nicer—and much easier to keep clean.

A Quick Review of Hard Floor Care

Most hard floors are maintained in much the same way. The basic principle of good floor care is to remove dirt and debris from it promptly, and whenever possible provide the flooring with a finish or wax that will protect it and from which dirt can easily be cleaned. All floors will deteriorate if not cleaned regularly.

Vinyl or Linoleum

All vinyl and even "no-wax" floors should have a coat of wax or polish applied so that dirt and debris from foot traffic won't damage them. Keep such floors dust-mopped and damp-mopped regularly, even if "they don't look dirty." Damp-mop with a mild all-purpose cleaner when soiled; rewax regularly in the traffic patterns.

Wood

Make sure wood floors are sealed with a good resinous or polyurethane "membrane" finish so moisture and stains won't penetrate the wood. Then treat wood floors like any hard flooring. Sweep, dust-mop, and damp-mop to maintain, but go light on the water, and don't let it puddle on the surface. Remove liquid spills immediately.

Laminate

Mop with plain water or water and vinegar only. Avoid using harsh or abrasive cleaners or cleaning tools. Don't use dust treatment if dust-mopping. No wax or floor finish is ever needed.

Concrete

Raw concrete will "bleed" dust and sand. Once interior concrete has cured, it should be cleaned thoroughly, allowed to dry, and then sealed with a concrete seal. The resulting protective finish can be maintained like other hard floors. Never paint concrete floors, because most paints will peel and chip off concrete.

Glossy or Matte-Finish Tile, Stone

The dozens of types of tiles available make it difficult to recommend a single method. If you have one of the more porous kinds of tile and are unhappy with it, ask the dealer (or your local janitorial-supply store) if there is a sealer or finish appropriate for your kind of tile. Remember that tiles intended to have a highly textured or "rustic" look will never shine no matter what—so don't waste your time and energy. Most stone or brick should not have wax or sealer applied.

Chapter Eleven

How to Clean Carpets for a Softer Life

"**N**ever shampoo a carpet before you have to, because once you do, it will get dirty faster" (Old Wives' Tales, continued). That's like saying, "Never wash your socks after the first wearing, because they'll get dirty faster." There are plenty of soothsayers around quoting great carpet wisdom to the home cleaner—most of which costs you time and money. With some simple professional techniques, you can get the job done, keep your carpets looking sharp, and minimize your maintenance time. My company cleans and maintains millions of square feet of carpet every night. What I've learned in the process applies to household as well as commercial carpeting.

Buy Quality Carpet

"Which carpet is best?" If I had a dollar for every time I've been asked that, I could carpet the parking lot at your favorite mall! Carpet is so much better today than it was twenty or thirty years ago. If you stick to a good, reputable dealer and a Stain-master or other soil-resistant type, it'll be hard to go wrong. The fierce competition in the carpet industry has forced the quality up; the majority of it is nylon now and stain-resistant, and it's good! Don't look for a bargain-basement price—better carpet is better, period! Pay the few extra dollars per yard to get the better grade, and have it installed professionally. You'll get thousands of dollars of benefit in comfort, durability, enjoyment, and ease of maintenance. Choose what you like, but make sure you get the good stuff.

Selecting carpet color, style, and material is generally a personal privilege, but living with it (especially maintaining it) may not be a "privilege" if you don't choose wisely. For example, commercial carpets are so tightly woven and low-pile they're now referred to as "soft floors," not carpeted floors. Don't get too commercial-minded and buy the "wear like iron" style. Believe me, it *feels* like iron when you roll around on it with the kids or tackle a "living room floor" project. Go for the highest-quality domestic instead, and you'll be better off all around. The feel and the look are a large part of the value of home carpeting. Much indoor-outdoor carpet is diffi-cult to maintain, not because it gets any dirtier than a thicker, plusher carpet, but because of its short pile and the solid colors it often comes in. Every tiny piece of litter or trash is highly visible on it, and little bits of thread and similar mate-rial resist being vacuumed off; a deep pile hides just about anything, from crumbs to catcher's mitts. This can be helpful on those days when company's coming and there's no time to clean. A homeowner will often spend hours selecting an exact shade of carpeting, not realizing that once it's in place and in use—under different light conditions, and underfoot being soiled—the color won't be the same as the color you chose for even a tenth of the time the carpet is in service. But color is one area where you should be cautious. There's no way you can keep airborne soil particles from industrial burning, home heating, and family cooking, or every bit of foot-borne debris from any carpet. All carpets will get soiled with time. Light gold, whites, yellow, or other pastel colors will serve you well if you live "el plusho" and your house is mainly a showplace. However, if you have children, grandchildren, pets, or lots of other visitors tramping through, those elegant light carpets will be a disaster. Light solid colors show soil and are difficult to shampoo, and often show "cow trails" (traffic paths). Patterned, textured, and multicolor carpets tend to hide soiling and wear.

Use common sense when you choose carpeting. Think of the maintenance. Deep pile is harder to vacuum than medium pile. Although the old classic, wool, is lovely, nylon, olefin, and other synthetics are far more stain resistant, durable, and easily cleaned. Oriental, Indian, and woven rugs must *always* be cleaned professionally. These and other area rugs *cause* housework because area rugs present two surfaces (instead of one) to clean. They're always being kicked and wrinkled, and they're easy to trip over. But they *are* beautiful. If you have to have them, hang them on a wall.

Kitchen and Bathroom Carpet

Never have carpet in a bathroom. There is 100 percent chance that moisture of all kinds will get on the carpet, as will hair spray and other grooming residue. The carpet will stink, harbor germs, grow mildew, and look ugly. Bathroom carpeting takes much more time to care for than hard-surfaced flooring, and it deteriorates rapidly. Don't do it!

And in the kitchen? Where bread always falls jelly-, mayonnaise-, or salami-side–down? Where meat juices run over the edge of the counter and dirty dishwater splashes out of the sink? Where pots of potato chowder overflow and casseroles of baked beans are dropped? Don't you have better things to do than clean carpet?

High-abuse areas such as bathrooms, kitchens, garages, studios, and workshops should have the lowest-maintenance, easiest-to-clean flooring possible. It will save you much time and grief, and money as well.

(If you're in doubt anywhere here, take a look at the book my daughter Laura and I did, called *Make Your House Do the Housework*, which covers carpet from every angle for looks, durability, and ease of upkeep.)

Regular Maintenance Is Important

Carpet in a home or lightly trafficked commercial building is easier to take care of than a hard floor if it's maintained properly. Its biggest problem is neglect. A carpet that looks okay is often used to the point of abuse, and this goes unnoticed until it's too late, when the owner of neglected carpet says, "I can't remember what color it used to be. It must be time to clean it." At this stage, most people wake up to the fact that carpets have to be maintained. But cleanup attempts are generally disappointing, and the owner becomes displeased with the carpet, unjustly blaming the problems on the salesperson or manufacturer.

You might think that carpet wear and damage result only from foot traffic. Wrong! Excessive carpet wear results from a combination of foot traffic, furniture pressure, and residues (such as sand and grit) that are allowed to remain in the carpet. Any sharp, abrasive particles or articles on or at the base of the carpet fibers are ground against the fibers as the carpet is walked on. In time, the fibers that aren't cut or damaged are soiled. The carpet wears out and gets soiled from the bottom as well as the top. Thus, to maintain your carpet properly, you've got to keep off or remove surface litter, dust, grit, wet soils, and airborne soils before they become embedded in your carpet. Another reminder: Good matting will eliminate a big share of this, especially wet soils and grit. Airborne dust you have to live with. Litter you can pick up or vacuum. The real culprit is embedded dirt.

Enter the Vacuum . . .

Vacuum cleaners were invented to efficiently remove not just surface dust and debris but embedded dirt from carpets. Few vacuums make as much impression on the carpet as they do on the user, who thinks noise, chrome, and suction are the ultimate. For ages, vacuum salespeople (all equal in wind velocity to their products) have unloaded shiny, overpriced machines on customers fascinated by suction and attachments. Neither of these is that important in maintaining your carpet and saving yourself housecleaning hours. After showing you how a vacuum can do everything but brush your teeth, the salesperson often drops a steel ball on the floor and picks it up with the vacuum. The gullible potential customer thinks, "If that vacuum can get a big steel ball off the carpet, sand and gravel will be a snap!"

Wrong! First, the steel ball trick is a maneuver that any vacuum, weak or strong, old or new, can do under the right conditions. Just get a steel ball slightly smaller than the hose and the ball is easily slurped up. Now take a piece of thread and mash it onto the carpet so it has a little static bind. A vacuum cleaner strong enough to pick up a piano bench will often have trouble picking up the thread because there's no "displacement lift." We've all tried to get up a thread, haven't we? Likewise, suction alone won't remove the embedded particles of dirt, grit, and sand. It will remove only the surface soil because, as with the thread, the displacement lift isn't there. The carpet fibers stand in the way, holding the embedded dirt, grit, and all those other villains grinding away at your carpet. A good "beater brush" vacuum is what's needed to pull all of this out of the pile.

Beat It!

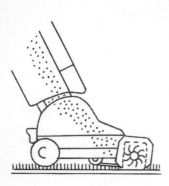

You can distinguish a vacuum with a beater brush or brush roll by the rapidly rotating brush that beats, combs, and vibrates the carpet. This loosens and dislodges embedded dirt and soil so the suction can pull it up into the vacuum. Most beater-brush heads will adjust to different heights and won't wear out carpet under normal use. On canister vacuums the brush roll is usually contained in a "power wand" type of attachment.

Which Vacuum?

A vacuum is indeed "the" tool of cleaning. There are hundreds of vacuums in all shapes and sizes—and a lot of them are excellent. A lot of them are also too big, too small, or too expensive. Many fill some special need better than another, but for all-around, all-purpose use in a home we want one that's easy to use, maintain, and repair.

I've used uprights at work and at home for more than fifty years. Ideally, you should buy two vacuums: first an upright beater-brush type. (I hate canister-type vacuums that drag behind you like a ball and chain.) I recommend a professional-quality upright, which is almost like the regular model—except it generally has a stronger motor, longer cord, a heavy-duty beater brush or brush roll, a more durable turn-on switch, and better quality bags. Some of them also have sensors that can tell the difference between carpet and hard flooring so the vac can adjust accordingly, and so that they can judge carpet nap height for more effective vacuuming. Just be sure you choose a model you feel comfortable handling. You should be able to buy a first-class pro upright for $300 to $450. Two brands I trust are Windsor and Eureka.

The old boxful of extra attachments that tended to be shuffled from closet to closet until the box wore out has been replaced on many uprights now by onboard tools that do all of the other things we like a vacuum to do besides vacuum carpet. Do be sure to get a vacuum with a long cord—who among us has not wished a hundred times that the vacuum cord was "just 10 feet longer"? An extension cord is a pain and cuts your efficiency greatly.

Commercial uprights are available with either cloth or disposable paper bags; many have a cloth bag that zips open so you can replace the paper bag inside. Disposables can be changed quickly, and they don't make a mess when you do. Disposables can be popped out and put right into the trash. In seconds, you're back on the road again. The vacuums that offer HEPA filtration are a big help for people with allergies or breathing difficulties. But a HEPA system is not worth the extra money, and will not do the job, unless all of the air exhausted from the cleaner goes through the filter.

If you use good doormats, you'll cut down vacuuming intake considerably, but it's still important to empty bags when they're no more than half full. When bags get too clogged, you'll smell dust when you click the vacuum on. If you see dust pouring out when you start up the vacuum, you've waited too long.

The Wet-Dry Vacuum

For your second machine, invest in a tank-type wet-dry vacuum. You'll be money and time ahead. A wet-dry is a vacuum that can safely be used to pick up both dry material and liquids. Generally this is accomplished by a simple filter adjustment. Wet-drys are great! They are the vacuums to buy a few attachments for, and the first one should be an extra long hose.

A wet-dry will not only clean up floods and spills and empty the old fish tank water, it's great for carpet edges, drapes, floors,

furniture, rafters (another reason for a long hose), car upholstery, campers, boats . . . the list could go on and on.

A small (ten-gallon capacity) wet-dry is the best size for
the household. Those twenty-gallon units will tempt you, but
stay with the small—remember, you'll be carrying it full of
toilet overflow or other unpleasant liquids better not slopped
out of the tank when you go to empty it. And getting out and
muscling around a jumbo wet-dry is a job you'll start wanting
to dodge. Wet-drys range in price from $49.95 on sale to more
than $100, or you can go high society and get a deluxe stain-
less steel tank type at a local janitorial-supply store for several
hundred dollars. When your neighbors and relatives see what
a wet-dry can do, you'll have to buy them one for their birth-
days, so shop accordingly!

Special-Purpose Assistants

The following helpers make special vacuuming jobs a snap:

- *Hand vacuums:* You can't beat these for quick pickup of
  little messes like a few cracker crumbs on the couch or
  the litter the kitty kicked out of the box. We're much
  more likely to clean it up now if we don't have to get out
  a whole big vacuum rig and plug it in. There are even
  hand-helds with beater bars that can handle things like
  embedded stair tread grit.
- *Wide-track vacuums:* These have wider heads (such as a 16
  inches instead of the usual 11 or 12), so you can zoom
  over the carpet in no time. If you have a big home with
  lots of carpet, they can cut a third off your vacuuming
  time. This is one secret that janitors with their acres of
  carpet have known for years.
- *Backpack vacuums:* Though these don't usually have a beater
  head or bar to help loosen dirt, for routine cleaning of hard
  and soft floors and high places, they're great. We pros use

them when cleaning in tight quarters where you can't be pushing or dragging a vacuum around. These do have to be plugged in, but they strap to your back and give you much greater freedom of movement in your cleaning operations.

Cord Control

Two ways we pros keep vacuum cords out of the way: (1) Hold the cord in your free hand, or (2) drape it over your shoulder and vacuum your way into a room or area instead of going all the way in and then vacuuming out (fighting the cord all the way).

Built-in Vacuum Systems

These beauties—also called "central vacs"—are still one of the best-kept secrets on the market.

My first experience with a built-in vacuum came when I opened a closet in a house we were cleaning. At first I thought I was looking at a giant coiled python ready to strike, but soon realized it was just the longest vacuum hose I'd ever seen. "Wow, there must be some hunk of vacuum to fit this baby," I thought. The owner later showed me the little wall receptacle where the hose inserted and turned into an instant vacuum. In the next year or so I only encountered a few more, but the more I saw of them, the more I liked them. And all of their owners seemed to be in love with them.

Installation is what most of us wonder about, but the vacuums fit easily in new homes and without much difficulty in the already-built ones. Dealers have videotapes to show you how to install them yourself, or they will do it for you. A central vac averages around $1,200 installed, but that's a bargain considering the time and energy it'll save over the years. I put one in my low-maintenance home in Hawaii and in my twenty-five-year-old masonry home. If you need a source, write to me at the address on page 49 and I'll send you a list of companies that can direct you to local distributors.

Here are the pluses of the central vac:

1. The suction of a central vac is significantly stronger, since it has a stronger motor than portable vacs.
2. It's the cleanest vacuum going. All of the dust and dirt as well as the air that is vacuumed up from the house is transported out of the room to a central collection area.
3. Since the motor is far away in the basement or garage, it's amazingly quiet.
4. All you handle is a light hose (you don't have to lug a heavy vacuum out), so it's super easy to use, especially for those once-a-day pickups or once-overs.
5. It saves wear and tear on the house (the vacuum hitting furniture legs and baseboards, etc.).
6. It's a permanent investment. You can buy one regular vacuum after another and end up with nothing to show for it, but installing a built-in is like putting money in the bank.

The nicest thing about central vacs is their simplicity—no vacuum to drag out, no canister to drag around, no cord to keep flipping over furniture (or pulling out of the socket). Central vacs also have *lots* of power, so don't go sticking the hose on your skin to test the suction.

Installing a Central Vacuum

The hose of the central vac is a little awkward if it's too long; be sure to put in plenty of receptacles so you can use a short hose.

With your central vac, too, you'll want beater-brush action to bounce dirt out, and the manufacturers do make a beater-brush head for the hose. If you get the air-driven type of beater head you won't have to worry about needing an electrical outlet at or near each receptacle to plug the power head into. Be sure to put a couple of outlets in the garage and anyplace you have stairs.

Put the receptacle in the garage near the exterior door, as three-quarters or more of your vehicle vacuuming will be done in the driveway, not in the garage.

Finally, be sure to mount all the receptacles and switches high—it'll save a lot of bending over.

A Vacuuming in Time . . .

Clean carpets look and feel better, and they last longer. A regularly maintained carpet means less-frequent shampooing, less time expended on carpet care, a longer life for the carpet, and more compliments from your guests!

The ideal carpet care plan is to:

1. Keep all possible dust, dirt, and abrasive material from getting on the carpet—the job of good matting.
2. Regularly remove all surface dirt and debris and extract harmful embedded debris from the carpet—the job of a good vacuum.
3. Keep grime cleaned off the top of the carpet so that it doesn't have a chance to penetrate—the job of effective surface cleaning.
4. Remove spots and spills immediately—your job! (See pages 161-162.)

Install a good set of mats as explained in Chapter 8, and vacuum carpets and mats regularly. Don't wait until you can see the dirt. Just because it's possible to camouflage crumbs, dog biscuits, pins, pennies, and peelings in deep pile doesn't mean you should overdo it. Keep all materials detrimental to carpeting out of the carpet. I've seen homes go for ten years before the carpets needed shampooing—all due to good matting and regular maintenance. Avoiding unnecessary shampooing is wise because shampooing is expensive whether you do it yourself or have it done professionally.

Professional Secrets of Better, Faster Vacuuming

Always police the area first to get any large debris off the carpet. A quick bend to pick up an object by hand is a lot faster and smarter than wasting ten minutes—and who knows how much repair shop money—trying to dig it out of your vacuum.

When possible, plug in to a strategic location that will allow you to vacuum the maximum area and avoid backtracking.

You don't have to vacuum every square inch every time. Spend most of your time on the traffic areas—that's where the dirt really is. Under and behind furniture and other out of the way or unused areas can go for two weeks or more without hurting a thing (including your honor). Likewise, don't sweat the edges—where the vacuum won't reach and the foot never treads. Once every two weeks or so, before vacuuming, sweep along the baseboards to flick out anything there to where the vacuum can reach it. Occasionally run over the corners and edges with your canister vac and crevice tool or dusting brush. Any dirt (mostly dust) there won't wear out the carpet, since we don't walk along the walls.

Slow, deliberate strokes pick up better and are faster in the end than zipping over one area three or four times. Let the vacuum work for you. It needs time for the beater bar to loosen the dirt, and for the airflow to suck it up. If you watch people vacuum, you'll see that a lot of time is often spent in overlap. This is a waste of time if you have a beater-brush assembly on your vacuum. Overlap each stroke an inch or so, but avoid running the machine over the same area twice, except as might be needed in badly soiled, high-traffic areas.

If you have a room that's especially dirty, you may have to resort to overlapping, up and back vacuuming strokes. But this takes a lot of time, tires you out, and usually isn't necessary. In rooms or halls that are too small for effective maneuvering, push the vacuum to the end of the stroke and then pull it back to cover the next strip of carpet. After you've pulled the vacuum all the way back, push it forward again and repeat the process. This method is quick and will do an effective job 90 percent of the time.

Unless it is designed for hard floors as well as carpets, always keep your vacuum on carpeted area while it's running. I've ruined a beautiful wood floor by running a low-adjusted beater-bar type vacuum over it. The metal part of the bar thumped the floor on every rotation and dented it (at great expense to me, since our insurance covers liability but not stupidity).

Stairs

Don't get on your hands and knees—vacuum the center traffic areas of the steps with your beater-brush vacuum. This will remove even deeply embedded dirt. As for the edges and corners that rarely are tread upon, just wipe with a damp cloth to pick up the visible surface dust, and occasionally hit 'em with a dust brush attachment when you do the edges in the rest of the house.

Area or Throw Rugs

Take area or throw rugs to a nearby carpeted floor for vacuuming. If you stand on one end of the rug and vacuum away from you, it won't get sucked in.

Vacuuming Carpet Fringe

Those fringes on area rugs and carpets are just lying there, waiting to be sucked up and jam your beater brush. Outsmart them by quickly sweeping them out of the way (over onto the rug they're attached to); then you can run your vacuum past the edges and pull up that previously hidden dust and dirt. Or you can bleed off the vacuum suction (that means open the little valve on the hose of a canistervac so the vacuum won't have as much suction). It will then pull up the dust bunnies, but not the fringes. (You can use the suction adjustment when you vacuum drapes, too.)

Vacuum carpeted stairways regularly; the corners only need to be wiped with a damp cloth occasionally.

Don't Abuse Your Vacuum

Eighty percent of vacuuming problems are caused not by a loose nut on the machine, but by the loose nut running it. The personality and habits of the user can take a great toll on vacuums. For example, I gave two heavy-duty pro vacuum cleaners for Christmas one year—one to my mother-in-law and one to another relative. My mother-in-law's vacuum still looked and worked like new twenty-six years later. The other one lasted less than thirteen months.

The unintentional (or sometimes intentional) vacuuming of coat hangers, paper clips, marbles, overshoes, and scissors is what hurts vacuums. Those clicks and clanks you hear when the vacuum picks up one of these or similar articles often means the (usually plastic) blades of the little gizmo in many uprights that generates suction—called the impeller or the turbulator fan—are being sheared off. It's not uncommon to have a vacuum run fine but without any suction, and a beat-up fan is generally the reason. (If it's not the fan, then it's probably the beater brush.) If you're vacuuming more and enjoying it less (getting up less dirt), you should probably replace the fan.

Note: A strong bar magnet screw-mounted to the front of your upright vacuum will pick up tacks, pins, needles, scissors, can openers, or any other metal object you might miss before vacuuming. It will save injuries to prowling pets, wrestling kids, and nice, new vacuum cleaners. Magnets like these are available from janitorial-supply stores, or the Cleaning Center.

Never feel under a beater vacuum to see if it's working.

Vacuum Health Checkup

The biggest secret of efficient vacuuming is keeping your vacuum well maintained. Your vac is your second most important set of wheels, so take care of it and check it regularly, just like your car.

- *Don't let your bag "overeat."* Anything more than 50 percent full will sap your vacuum's cleaning energy and strain the motor.
- *Never run over the cord or pinch it in doorways.* Avoid using extension cords; they lower your vacuum's performance.
- *Protect the plug.* Remove it from the receptacle with your fingers, not by pulling on the cord.

- *Tighten the screws in the handle every so often or they'll work loose and fall off.* Keep the handle clean—it's easier to grip, and more sanitary, too.

- *Keep the rubber bumper in place* to protect your vacuum as well as your furniture and baseboards.

- *Make sure the brushes on the beater brush or brush roll aren't worn to nubs* (if they are, you can slip in a new brush insert—it's easy). Check the beater occasionally for cracks or jagged edges that can snag carpet pile.

- *The right pile adjustment on your vacuum gives the beater brush room to move to loosen deep dirt.* It also ensures that the suction will be able to carry the debris into the bag. Set the brush to its highest setting, completely up off the floor, and turn the vacuum on. Lower the setting gradually until you hear the brush come in light contact with the carpet. If you set it lower than that ("I'm really gonna chomp the carpet"), you cut off the air flow and slow down the beater. Some vacs have automatic sensors to take care of pile adjustment.

- *Make sure the belt is tight and that it's on right. If it's worn, replace it.* Don't buy cheap imitation belts—only genuine original manufacturer's parts for your make and model. If the belt runs hot, clean the motor pulley of threads, glaze, and accumulated dirt.

- *Make sure the brush roll turns easily and is free of thread, string, and shoelaces.* String wrapped around the bar will pressure the bearings and cause them to turn harder and even heat up. Hooking the point of scissors under them is the best way to remove things like this.

- *If you seem to have a lot less suction these days, have a vacuum repair shop check the fan.* The fan is what creates the suction, and the blades might be worn down or broken. For a few dollars you'll have your vac like new again. Speaking of new vacuums, when you get your next one look for one such as the Windsor with a bypass airflow system, designed so that dirt and debris you pick up with the vac doesn't go past the fan and possibly harm it.

- *Dust the exterior of the machine,* and wipe off the power cord and handle occasionally!

Soil Retardant

If your carpeting isn't one of the newer types with soil resistance built right into the fibers, it's a good idea to treat it with soil retardant. A soil retardant is a chemical treatment that helps carpets resist soiling and helps prevent water and soil-based spots and spills from becoming hard-to-remove stains. Water-based soiling agents, such as soda, milk, coffee, mud, and winter slush cause big maintenance problems as they soak into carpet fibers and backing, rapidly deteriorating appearance. Soil retardant can be applied to clean carpet, old or new. It's often applied during manufacture, so chances are your new carpet has it. (Ask, when you buy a carpet.)

The best-known brands of soil retardant are Scotchgard and Teflon. If applied correctly, they can be a real boon. After spending time in the 3M testing labs observing control blocks of carpet treated with Scotchgard versus untreated, I was impressed. **You can apply Scotchgard yourself following the directions on the container, or have your dealer do it for you.** You can even purchase carpet and upholstery shampoo containing Scotchgard.

Just because carpet is protected by a soil retardant doesn't mean you can forget about it. You must still keep up your regular schedule of cleaning and maintenance. The chemical types of soil retardant have to be reapplied every time you deep clean (shampoo) the carpet. Carpets with soil protection locked right into the fibers themselves must be cleaned according to the manufacturer's instructions, or you can undo their stain resistance and void the warranty.

Antistatic Agents

Static electricity is the mild shock produced when you touch a metal object after walking across a carpet. It's the result of friction. While not harmful (except possibly to delicate electronics), it can be irritating. And static electricity can actually pull dust particles from the air. By eliminating static, you keep your carpet cleaner.

Some carpeting contains a small amount of stainless steel fiber to dissipate static electricity. For carpeting that lacks this feature, applying an antistatic agent to the carpet periodically or simply increasing the humidity in the room can help the problem.

Spots and Stains

Spots, stains, and spills on carpet are just as upsetting in the home as they are in the commercial buildings I clean. It's important to the health and beauty of your carpet to clean up spots and spills as soon as possible.

You should keep at least two different spot removers on hand—an all-purpose spotter for water-based substances (food, blood, etc.) and a solvent spotter for tar, grease, and oil stains. If a particular problem keeps recurring in your household, you may want to have some additional products on hand—bacteria/enzyme digester, for example, if you have pet "accidents" or children in toilet training. These spotters are available at janitorial-supply stores and elsewhere, and are very effective. If there's a stain they won't remove, you can call in a professional, who will get the spot out chemically or doughnut-cut that piece of carpet and plug in a new piece.

Remember: Keep cleaning solutions and tools safely out of reach of little children. Store your spot removal tools

and supplies in a small plastic carrying tray. This will
organize your supplies for quick attack on spots.

It's important before you try to deal with it to know what
a stain or mark on the carpet *is*. What base is it—water or
oil? You must match the base of the stain to the base of the
cleaner—for instance, a water-based detergent solution won't
make much of an impact on oil, but a petroleum-based solvent spotter will dissolve it immediately.

Smelling and feeling a spot will help you determine what it
is. You can also ask other household members (nicely!) if they
know anything about how the spot got there. If a spot is darker
than the carpet, you have a chance of removing it; if it's lighter,
that means the substance bleached the fibers and the spot will
need to be plugged (unless you can rearrange the furniture).

Bleaching a stain, even with relatively mild bleach like
hydrogen peroxide, is a last resort, unless you want a little adven-
ture or a new *white* spot as a conversation piece. Before you bleach,
always test the carpet or fabric in an unobtrusive place.

Red stains—from barbecue sauce to Kool-Aid to melted
cherry popsicles—have always been among the worst. But now
there are special professional products designed just for this
purpose, so if you have a stubborn red blotch somewhere,
check with a janitorial-supply store or pro carpet cleaner.

Smart Spot Removal

1. Catch the spot or stain when it's fresh. Chances for removal are 75 percent better.
2. Carefully blot or scrape the entire stained area thoroughly before applying any solution. If the spot is very large, use your wet-dry vacuum. Avoid using liquids before you've blotted up all you can; they might spread the stain.
3. Before using any chemicals, test carpet in a small, inconspicuous area to make sure damage or discoloration won't occur.
4. Don't rub the spill; it might spread the problem. Work spot cleaner from the outside of the stain toward the inside to avoid spreading the stain.
5. After treatment, blot up all moisture. If you used a detergent or ammonia cleaning solution, rinse the spot with cool or lukewarm water. Blot again. Dry with a terry towel and brush the nap to a standing position after the stain is gone.
6. After your final blotting, if you feel there is still too much moisture, place a stack of terry cleaning cloths (see page 50) over the spot, and weight them with a heavy object. Leave overnight and then brush up the nap.

The critical difference in spot removal on carpet as opposed to other fabrics on hard surfaces is in the drying. Carpets are low and there's no such thing as air circulation under them, so whenever you wet them you need to pull out that moisture with a dry cloth (blot), or even a wet-dry vacuum if necessary. Get out all the moisture you can, and if it's still wet place a fan near the spot. If carpet stays damp it will rot, mildew, breed bacteria, smell, and the floor underneath can even warp and buckle!

If you have wool carpet or upholstery, try to avoid wet-cleaning it. Use dry-cleaning solvents whenever possible. Call your dealer for advice.

Be patient—give the chemicals time to work. Don't expect all stains to come out immediately—most take some time. Most old stains and spots can't be removed, and some chemical stains are permanent damage that can't be reversed, so don't get your hope up too high about that three-year-old acne medicine stain you've placed the night table over. It might have to remain until you replace the rug!

For complete stain removal instructions for even the toughest stains, see my book *Don Aslett's Stainbuster's Bible.*

Shampooing the Carpet

There comes a time in the life of all carpet—regardless of how faithfully you have vacuumed, removed spills and spots, and kept mats at the doors—that it will have collected enough dirt and soil deep in the pile that all of this just has to be washed or "shampooed" out. Some people shampoo the carpet every year (which is probably too often), and some do it once they can see the carpet start to twitch and move by itself. The grime usually sneaks up on us, like a few extra pounds on us, or weeds in the garden—by the time we realize it, we've waited too long. A carpet's location, color, and the amount of traffic it receives will have a lot to do with when it needs to be cleaned, but there are several ways to determine when shampooing is needed:

1. Look for a clean place (under the couch, a saved remnant, etc.) and compare it with the rest of the carpet.
2. Feel it! Dirty carpet feels heavy, matted, and sticky.
3. Rub the carpet with a white towel dampened with carpet shampoo (or plain water). The dirt and soil will show up like a red flag.

4. Smell it. Musty, dusty carpet has a smell we all know too well. Get down on your knees and sniff a few times.

5. You can see a 3-foot grimy circle around the TV chair or a dust storm follows you when you walk across the carpet!

. . . Okay, it's ready! Besides that, company is coming, and you're holding your daughter's wedding reception at home. You have two basic choices to get the job done: Do it yourself, or call a professional. (And once it's clean, start a regular surface-cleaning program—see page 169.)

I'm the first to push independence and doing things yourself, but I caution you about the pitfalls of shampooing your own carpet. It's not necessarily a complicated job, but don't be deceived by the propaganda of trouble-free money-saving automatic, do-it-all machinery. The operator of the machine has to have some knowledge, the ability to adapt to different carpet-cleaning requirements, and understand how much moisture and chemical to use. Otherwise a poor cleaning job, overwetting, or fiber and backing damage will result. It amazes me that people will spend $2,500 for a carpet, and then attack it with powerful cleaning gear without any experience whatsoever.

Another pitfall is cost-value miscalculation. Take, for example, a 14 × 20-foot living room carpet, which a professional might shampoo for $30. A pair of homeowners (who are missing out on a fishing trip) will drive ten miles across town to rent a big steamer or rug outfit for $20 or more. Then they'll buy $10 to $15 worth of chemicals, scrape up the family car getting it all in, and drive another ten miles home. They'll unload the heavy equipment, grunting and groaning. Then they'll move furniture, read directions, spend most of Saturday cleaning carpet, and will probably have to drive back for more shampoo.

Once they've finished, it's a repeat performance of loading and driving to return the equipment. At the end of the day, they've spent $35 on gas, rent, shampoo, etc.—not to mention their time. They are dead tired; have experienced one smashed hand, three arguments, two dog versus cat fights; they're disappointed with the results—and, come Sunday night, the carpet still isn't dry in places.

I've cleaned carpets for fifty years, so I always do my own because I know how to and have easy access to the equipment. But I would never do my own if I had to round up and rent the mediocre machines available to the average person and go through all that. I couldn't afford it and wouldn't enjoy the hassle.

If you insist on doing it yourself, see pages 167 to 169 for some ways to improve your results.

Professional Carpet Cleaning

There are also pitfalls to having your carpet cleaned by the professionals. Not all so-called professionals are professionals. Some "carpet cleaners" are opportunists who were franchised or hired for a big kill; their training has been by trial and error.

The method used in shampooing carpets is important. That TV before-and-after demonstration of a great contrast once a little foamy carpet shampoo is rubbed on is deceptive. That isn't cleanliness you behold, but the "optical brightening" most carpets exhibit when wetted. **After a light foam job, many carpets appear to gleam and sparkle, but they can still be filthy.**

This has been the story with much home carpet-cleaning and is, in fact, the reason you so often hear: "Never shampoo your carpets, for once you do, they will get dirty faster." They *do* get dirty faster, but only because the surface was grazed with a dab of shampoo, and the moisture carried the dirt and soap down to the bottom of the fibers, only to emerge quickly when the carpet is in use again. Also, many shampoos leave a soil-attracting residue on the carpet fibers.

You will be approached by mail or by phone about the "mist" method, the "foam" method, the "dry-powder" method, and the "steam" or "extraction" method. Be cautious of any of these on your carpets because they are all in some way ineffective. For example, "steam" isn't what it's cracked up to be, but when steam cleaning hit the market, it positively revolutionized carpet cleaning. It wasn't the steam itself but the extraction process that was so valuable: Hot cleaning solution is pressure-injected into the carpet, and a superstrong wet vacuum immediately pulls almost all the moisture back out.

It's my opinion that steam extraction alone generally won't clean an old, dirty carpet. The water extracted from the carpet is impressively muddy, but remember that the time between the solution's being injected and removed is so brief that it can't dissolve much of the goop adhering to the fibers. Rotary motion or scrubbing action is needed after the solution is applied to loosen all the dirt and deep clean the carpet. This should be followed by extracting (rinsing) to remove all dirt, soap, etc.

Great Deals?

If you do decide to have your carpets done rather than do them yourself, first make sure there's a good, professional carpet cleaner in your area. (*Always* check references.)

Be sure to get a firm price quote. And ask which method they use. If they say "steam" or "extraction," request a truck-mounted unit that heats the solution to 150°F and has the power to actually steam-clean your carpet. Make sure that they are going to pretreat and prespray any stains.

If they say "rotary," make sure that after they've scrubbed the carpet it is rinsed with hot water by the extraction method. That means, if nine gallons of liquid go into the carpet, they get eight-and-a-half gallons back out. Some professionals call the combination of rotary scrubbing and hot water extraction "showcase" cleaning. It's the most expensive but does the best job.

How to Do a Better Job if You Do it Yourself

All kinds of places carry rental shampoo equipment, from the simplest to the two-gorilla size guaranteed to beat up your car and give you a hernia loading and unloading. Companies such as Bissell and Sears also sell scaled-down hot-water extraction units.

Equipment like this doesn't have the horsepower to truly deep clean the carpet all the way down to the roots—the suction isn't strong enough and the water doesn't get hot enough. These units are probably better suited for surface cleaning (see page 169). If you follow the manufacturer's directions, the best you can expect is a fair job of shampooing.

Whether you use them to surface-clean or shampoo, you can do a couple of important things with a small extractor that will double your shampooing speed and efficiency.

The filthy water you see coming out of the carpet when you're using an extractor gives the illusion that your carpet is really getting cleaned, but that dirty water is just the easy surface dirt that comes off as soon as the carpet is wet. The little sprayers shoot the solution into the carpet, but before the solution can attack the tough, stuck-on-dirt—the aged dog doo, the smashed raisins, the ground in jellybeans—the vacuum pulls it back out. We pros call this problem not enough "dwell time"; in other words, the solution isn't in the fibers long enough to exert any chemical action, only to dissolve the loose, easy dirt.

The good professional carpet cleaner using an extractor system does one of the following, any of which you can do:

1. *Scrub the carpet briefly before you start to extract,* using a rotary floor scrubber or "buffer," or even just by hand with a cleaning cloth or towel. Just dip the cloth into some shampoo foam (not lots of water) and work that into the carpet to attack and emulsify the dirt clinging to the carpet yarn. When you follow that with the extractor, shooting hot

water into the carpet and pulling it out, it's like a flushing rinse—a lot more of the dirt comes out, a lot faster.

2. *Use a carpet prespray solution at least five minutes before you start shampooing.* Lightly spray the carpet, using a hand spray bottle or even a weed-type sprayer if the job is a big one. You don't want to soak the carpet, just mist it to wet the surface, where most of the dirt and airborne oils are. Spray a little heavier in the traffic patterns, where the dirt is thicker and worked in. The solution will loosen and release the soil so that when you pass over it with your trusty extractor unit—snort, bobble, squeak—your water will really be dirty now, and you can sigh confidently that you do have most of the dirt.

3. *You can also use a two-step method* (your local janitorial-supply store will have everything you need to do this) of applying a stronger prespray over the whole carpet, leaving it on for three to five minutes, and then going over the whole carpet again with a rinse-neutralizer. This neutralizes any cleaning residue left in the carpet and prevents accelerated resoiling.

Protect carpet when shampooing. Block furniture legs with pieces of cardboard or waxed paper. If an imprint from the blocking material remains, rub the area with a bit of clear water. Brush up the carpet pile and let it dry.

Rental extractor units such as Rug Doctor have a little scrubber built into the head. Even with these it's better to first apply the solution lightly with the scrubbing tool but not the vacuum; then on the second trip, give it the full business, all controls on. This way you'll have given the shampoo time to "deterg the dirt."

If you do a lot of shampooing, go to a janitorial-supply store (or see page 49 for a mail-order source) and get a gallon of shampoo concentrate. It's much cheaper than the stuff they sell with the machines.

Surface Cleaning to Delay Shampooing

Most homeowners put up with increasingly dirty carpet until they can't stand it anymore—then they spring for an expensive steam-cleaning job. They could learn something from those who maintain carpeting in commercial buildings. Commercial cleaners have learned the value of regular surface cleaning to keep carpets looking good and to stretch out the time between deep cleaning. Surface cleaning is just what it sounds like—a spiffing up of the surface of the carpeting. Deep cleaning (such as extraction cleaning or shampooing) takes more time but cleans the carpet clear down to the base of the fibers.

A home extraction machine is just one way to surface-clean carpeting. Dry powders (Host, Capture, and Amway dry carpet cleaners are some good ones) can be applied by hand or with a purchased or rented machine that is specially designed to scrub them in; with many models you have to use a regular vacuum to remove the powder afterward. You can surface-clean a limited area of carpeting (such as a grimy spot near a doorway) by dipping a terry cleaning cloth into a light solution of carpet shampoo and water, wringing the cloth out well, and using it to gently wipe the dirty area. Leave the solution on there a few minutes, blot it out with a dry cloth, then follow with a damp-rinse of clean water on a cleaning cloth. Be careful not to scrub or you will frizz the pile.

A Few More Do-It-Yourself Carpet-Cleaning Cautions

- Vacuum well before you start.
- Don't let the solution sit too long before you extract it.

- Don't overwet! Keep the wand moving and only make one pass to wet the carpet. Overwetting can cause the backing and pad to rot, mildew, or even shrink.

- Use a good-quality shampoo in the recommended dilution. Using cheap shampoo or too much shampoo can cause rapid resoiling.

- Ventilate! Open some windows, if possible, or turn on a fan to help fumes dissipate and the carpet dry out.

- Long-napped carpet may need to be raked or swept to a stand-up position to dry.

- Let the carpet get good and dry before you walk on it again or replace the furniture.

Chapter Twelve

What to Do about Furniture

"How do I clean my furniture?" This is a question home cleaners ask me repeatedly. My own attitude toward furniture is "I dislike moving it, and I dislike buying it even more."

In an attempt to eliminate both my furniture frustrations, I designed out most of the furniture in a home we built in the resort mountains of Sun Valley, Idaho. Our living room had an octagonal conversation pit padded with vinyl cushions. Twelve or thirteen people could sit and visit comfortably. A plush, padded two-stair landing where ten or twelve more visitors could sit faced into the living room. This house didn't have a single piece of furniture except for the beds and the dining-room set. Our home was not only beautiful, but also usable for family and groups of up to forty, and I didn't have to buy or move furniture!

But for most of you, furniture not only must be bought and moved, it must be cleaned. So the question becomes,

"How do I keep my furniture looking nice without a lot of time and effort?"

Attempts to answer this question have greatly stimulated the sales of "miracle" furniture polishes. Think about the messages given by thousands of furniture polish commercials: "Fast and easy"; "polished clean and lint-free"; "see yourself reflected"; "Brand X will shine your dingy furniture better than Grandma's beeswax and turpentine—and it smells woody, lemony, and expensive."

Furniture care isn't that simple. There *are* some ways to cut the time spent caring for furniture and make it last longer. (Notice I said "ways," not "way.") It isn't done with a squirt of magic aerosol furniture polish as a TV or magazine ad might suggest.

My approach to furniture cleaning is more preventive than maintenance-oriented. Well-manufactured furniture, although it may be expensive to buy, costs less in the long run. Cheap furniture loses its crisp, elegant look rapidly and becomes conspicuously dull and shabby-looking. Once in this decrepit condition, it takes a lot of time and supplies to maintain it. And it rarely looks any better cleaned and polished than it did before you started. Select carefully and go for good quality. Paying a little more cash will save a lot of your most precious commodity: personal time.

Choosing Furniture with an Eye to Cleanability

The design and style of furniture you choose will determine how many hours per day, week, or year you will have to spend maintaining it. Elaborate decorations, carvings, and grooves take more time to keep looking good. And the more kinds of material furniture is made of (or a room is decorated with) the more time and types of equipment and supplies it will take to clean.

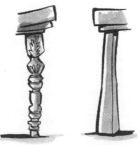

Which chair leg would you rather clean?

You are the sole judge on this one. If the décor of your home calls for the elaborate unit, you have to decide the long-range value of owning it. No matter what you have in mind, check the furniture and make sure all the surfaces *can* be maintained.

Wood should have a finish—not just an oiled surface or a colored stain, but a transparent varnish-type coat, called a "membrane finish," to prevent dirt and cleaning materials from penetrating into the wood. Natural or bare wood that needs constant "feeding" or oiling is a pain to maintain and will look dull and discolored before long. Lighter-toned wood furniture shows less dust and damage, is easier to make look good, and remains that way longer than darker furniture.

Metal should have a smooth finish, not be pitted or engraved. It should have baked enamel or other hard-surfaced coating. Stainless steel and chrome are durable, but require a lot of effort to keep clean and bright. Brushed chrome is better.

Glass used as an overlay on a desk or table looks good and doesn't show dust or fingerprints too badly. But clear glass see-through units—such as coffee tables and end tables—act like a magnifying glass. *Everything* shows—a piece of lint will look like a caterpillar.

Is It Cleanable?

Fabric tends to be the most used and abused part of furniture. Spillage on furniture is as common as on carpet, believe it or not. Some fabrics look superb, but stains and marks on them may never be removed. Soil retardants such as Scotchgard, which the manufacturer may apply or you can buy at the supermarket or hardware store and apply, is a lifesaver for most upholstery and for you personally. It is an excellent protection for most fabrics, making them more maintainable, because the fibers are protected from stains and soil.

If you have your heart set on wicker or cane, spray-enamel or spray-polyurethane it the minute you have it inside the door; this will make it somewhat cleanable (depending on what you spill on it).

Is It Restorable?

Some fabrics look great when new or newly cleaned, but after a few people sit on them, they become matted or shiny. After some velvet and velour-type materials have been sat on a rump print remains, and you have better things to do than go around brushing up cushions to make them look good. Pick a fabric that "restores," or comes back to life, after use (or that doesn't need to "restore"). Select a hard-finish fabric for dining-room chairs that are used constantly. White or light-colored fabrics (especially solid colors) show and accent every spot. Fabrics with some color blend or a pattern hide dirt better. Again, this is a matter of taste—but try to make it easy on yourself. Remember, furniture exists for your use and comfort.

Keeping Your Furniture Looking Nice

Convinced that the secret of furniture maintenance is in the bottle or can of polish, the majority of us use too much of it. We build up layers of gunk, which results in more work and sometimes even surface deterioration. A cloth that leaves no oil or residue and picks up dust is the best thing to use. This means that a microfiber cloth or washable electrostatic dust cloth is the way to go. You can also purchase treated paper dust cloths at your local janitorial-supply store. They're called Masslinn cloths, and they'll last and last; when they're dirt-saturated, you can throw them away.

The pro approach might give you new ideas about furniture cleaning. My company cleans thousands of desktops, tabletops, chairs, stands, racks, and cabinets every night throughout the United States. In most of our cleaning, we wipe with Masslinn cloths to remove dust. When finger- and handprints have to be removed, we use a light spray of all-purpose cleaner or a water-dampened cloth to wipe, and then dry-buff to a natural sheen. We avoid using polish where the finish can maintain its own luster. You could also use a solution of one of the oil soaps made for wood, followed by buffing with a dry cleaning cloth.

If you use an aerosol polish, use it seldom and lightly. Select one type of polish and use it consistently. The reason for this is simple: Often your furniture surfaces will come out dull and streaked because your new polish isn't compatible with the oil polish.

Types of Polish

- *Clear oil treatment:* Usually some kind of oil (mineral or vegetable) and solvent blend, this is used to "feed" bare wood. It has a wet, glossy look when applied, but a dull sheen after it soaks in. It will become an oily, sticky film if used on varnished or polyurethane-coated wood.
- *Liquid or paste solvent:* This is hard to apply, but it has excellent water and abrasion resistance. It is low gloss, but durable.
- *Oil emulsion polish:* A cream-type polish, it has the same drawbacks as clear oil.
- *Water or oil wax emulsion (aerosol or spray):* This type of polish contains a variety of waxes, silicones, and polymers, generally in a water base. It has all the components of a good polish: protects your furniture, enhances its beauty, and makes it easy to dust. Used once a year or so it is good, but if you use it every time you clean it'll lay a thick layer of gunk on your pretty wood.

If you have raw or natural wood surfaces in your home they'll need to be "fed," or treated to keep them from drying out and cracking. Rub on clear oil treatments such as lemon oil. Take your time so the wood can absorb the oil, and then wipe off the excess.

In my opinion, feeding wood is a waste of effort and material. Besides, if grease or ink gets on bare wood, it's ruined. Low-gloss or satin-sheen finishes that seal the surface are available; they form a glasslike membrane through which that beautiful grain will still be bright and clear and fully visible. Marks and stains will end up on the finish instead of on the wood.

If you wish to apply (or reapply) a varnish or polyurethane coat to ailing wood surfaces, it's easy. First, clean the surface with a strong cleaning solution—a strong ammonia solution, wax stripper, or degreaser if it's been sealed; solvent if it's raw wood—to take off all dirt and oils. Let it dry until any swollen grain goes down. Take care of any nicks or raised spots with a few strokes of superfine sandpaper, and then wipe with a tack cloth or a cloth very lightly dampened with paint thinner to pick up any dust or lint on the surface. Finally, apply the varnish or polyurethane, paying attention to the directions on the container. It may take two coats or even more to assure full coverage.

Dusting

One of the simplest ways to keep your furniture looking nice is to keep it dusted. The frequency with which you need to dust depends on how dusty or polluted your area is, how readily your furniture shows dust, and how finicky you are.

Dust causes more mental anxiety to you than it does physical damage to your dwelling, so don't get your duster feathers ruffled. Dust does little harm (except to our pride when someone visits) unless someone in the family is allergic to it. (Dust on floors, carpets, and electronic equipment however, *does* cause damage or deterioration.)

You can reduce dusting to a minor duty if:

- You place and maintain proper matting.
- Your vacuum works well and you use it. Empty your vacuum bag frequently, because if you vacuum when it's full you'll create dust.
- You clean or replace your furnace and/or air conditioner filters regularly.
- Your home is weatherproofed (door and window seals, caulking, etc.); weatherproofing keeps dust out, too.

When you dust, don't use clouds of aerosol polish or puddles of oily wood treatments, because after a while, you'll create a waxy or oily buildup that will look bad, be sticky and more difficult to clean, and actually attract and hold dust. Always dust *before* you vacuum so that the crumbs and Cheerios and orange seeds in the corners and crannies of the furniture won't end up on a neatly vacuumed floor. Dust high places first. This gets the dead flies and other debris off the ledges and onto the floor, from where it can be vacuumed easily.

Dusting Drill

1. Dust before you vacuum.
2. Work top to bottom.
3. A weekly once-over-lightly is enough for the average house.
4. Monthly, hit the door frames, window blinds, valances, and light fixtures.
5. Dust the lofts and rafters at least twice a year, using a lambswool duster on an extension handle.

Use the right dusting tool. Unless you are faced with a bunch of tiny or delicate things to dust, such as knickknacks, *don't* use a feather duster. The air movement a feather duster causes will blow particles all over and you'll chase dust for hours. Instead, use one or more of following tools.

You could use a Masslinn cloth. (This is the disposable chemically treated paper dust cloth mentioned earlier.) It picks up—in fact, it attracts!—dust and small particles and is excellent for fine furniture. It will snag on rough surfaces (but any surface that rough should be vacuumed). When a cloth becomes saturated with dust (after about three months of daily use in the average-sized dwelling), simply pitch it and use a new one. These cloths leave a nonsticky luster on wood and other finishes and they cost only pennies at janitorial-supply stores.

There are other types of electrostatic dust cloths, such as the Wonder dust cloth, that do an excellent job of dusting too. Electrostatic fabric, without any oil or treatment of any kind, picks up and holds dust and lint and even beetle eyebrows. When an electrostatic dust cloth gets filthy (which it does because everything clings to it), just toss it in the washer. It can be laundered and reused over and over—now *that's* a dust cloth!

Microfiber cloths, woven from threads that are only one-hundredth the size of a human hair, lift dust from surfaces and hold it tight until the cloth is washed in hot water, so they don't transfer dust from surface to surface. They're supersoft and pleasant to use, too.

A water-dampened soft terry cleaning cloth (see the equipment chart in Chapter 5) is another option. Make sure it's thoroughly wrung out so it's only slightly damp. A damp terry duster won't damage surfaces or create extra work; it will hold and remove dust and other residue. When you use one, be sure to keep switching to a clean side so it won't become a dust distributor. When it's dust-saturated, use another cloth. On glossy surfaces, use a dry, clean cloth to buff after the damp cloth.

A lambswool duster is a fluffy ball of (sometimes synthetic) wool on the end of a long handle. It looks like cotton candy on a stick, but almost magically picks up dust and fine particles by static attraction. It's especially good for dusting high and low cobwebs and Venetian or miniblinds. Shake it outside after use, and vacuum it when it gets dust-saturated. Lambswool dusters can be bought at a janitorial-supply or housewares stores, and are also available as duster heads that can be attached to an extension handle.

Cobwebs come off easily if you flick them off, rather than rub them in. The lambswool duster is the best tool for the purpose.

Becoming a Dust Detective

The big trick to dusting is learning where the dust collects: at the corners, tops, and bottoms of walls and furniture, light fixtures, wall hangings, and any horizontal surface. The greatest amount of dust isn't at eye level, as most of us imagine. Natural air currents in the house deposit dust and dirt 18 to 24 inches from the ceiling, and 2 or 3 feet up from the floor, and this happens even if no one is in the house! There's plenty of it down low where our feet kick things around and pets lounge, and where the fluff from higher-up settles. The floor (especially a carpeted floor) is full of it, and as we stir it up it lands on the lower rungs and lower half of furniture legs. Take a good look down there and you'll see.

Dust one room at a time with a lambswool duster. Hit the higher areas first, using the side of the duster like a large paintbrush, taking care to cover the whole surface and overlap a little. Don't forget those havens for dust known as screens and lattice that may look okay at first glance. Dust and cobwebs really snuggle in here; you have to look close. Even those who dust the top of the door-casing trim usually forget the inside of the frame down both sides of the door. Static electricity accumulates here as people, pets, and air pass through, so you'll usually see lots of fuzz there.

As for that low dusting: With that long handle on a lambswool duster, you hardly even have to bend at the belt. For dusting rough surfaces that might snag or tear a dust cloth or duster, use the dust brush of your vacuum.

Cleaning Fabric Upholstery

As part of your routine cleaning, keep both vinyl and fabric upholstery vacuumed. Go over the whole piece with the upholstery attachment of your vacuum. On sturdy fabrics that can take it (not vinyl or delicate fabrics), you can also use the power wand of a canister or even an upright vacuum itself. Slight surface dirt or hair and skin oils on fabric or vinyl can be removed with a cloth dampened by a carpet shampoo solution; then wipe with a damp rinse cloth and rub dry with a towel. This kind of surface removal works well if you do it often enough so that the headrest, armrests, and seat don't have a chance to get too dirty.

A surface spot on upholstery can be wiped or cleaned with an applicator dampened with cleaning solution and then dried with an absorbent cloth. Professional spotting kits with instructions are available from most large carpet distributors or a janitorial-supply store.

Things looking dim around the house? It may not be a reflection on your cleaning; it might just be dust, grime, and cigarette smoke coating your light bulbs. Fluorescent tubes, for example, lose 40 percent of their glow if they aren't kept clean; but the loss is so gradual you never notice. Dust and wash them today. (Be sure to turn the light off and let

the bulbs cool down first. A cloth dampened with all-purpose
cleaner should do it.) It'll brighten up the whole place.

When upholstery really gets dirty, you should call a professional so that it will be cleaned right. But it *is* possible to do
it yourself. Always be sure to check manufacturers' cleaning
instructions, or the tag on the furniture, which should indi-
cate whether or not the piece can be wet-cleaned.

Most lampshades can't really be cleaned. They're fairly delicate
and slowly deteriorate from the heat of the light bulb. Lampshades
are often stained, or the light has faded them or cooked dirt
onto them. If vacuuming, dry-sponging, and gently spotting
with solvent spotter won't work, go shopping for new ones!

If the fabric is thoroughly soiled, it should be washed
("shampooed") with an upholstery-cleaning solution or
shampoo, and then rinsed out—this is where problems arise
in a do-it-yourself upholstery-cleaning job. Cleaning solution
is scrubbed on the dirt and the upholstery fabric seems to
be cleaner. Actually, the surface dirt has been loosened and
has sunk deeper into the fabric along with the cleaning solution. The fabric appears clean, but it isn't. The fabric is soaked
with chemical, which leaves it sticky and matted. The dirt and
moisture have to be removed with an upholstery extractor
attachment or a good wet-dry vacuum. Soon after you apply
the cleaner, rinse with clear water and use the extractor again.
But be sure to use water sparingly—don't get the backing or
filling material wet! When cleaning upholstery, always use the
least aggressive method that gets results.

Some other things to remember include:

- Napped fabric should be brushed upright (all in the same direction) before it dries.
- If your upholstery has been treated with soil retardant, it will usually have to be reapplied after deep cleaning.

Appliances

One of the most important principles in cleaning appliances, as in any cleaning, is to keep them up. If you let your oven or refrigerator go without cleaning forever, of course it's going to be a depressing and time-consuming chore once you do decide to clean it.

People often correctly guess that can openers are one of the dirtiest places in the house, yet few ever clean them. If you have an electric one, unplug it, and then spray dish detergent solution onto the cutting and clamping area. Wait four or five minutes. Scrub with a vegetable brush and rinse. That will get the crud and bacteria, too!

Frequent, easy, spray-and-wipe cleanups will keep your kitchen appliances looking new indefinitely. Most appliances have an enamel surface: acrylic, porcelain, or baked. It's tough and stain-resistant, but not tough enough to resist abrasives. So don't use scouring cleanser, metal scrapers, or steel wool or abrasive (colored) nylon scouring pads on your appliances; these are damaging to enamel, stainless steel, chrome-plated metal, and plastic surfaces alike. Do use the following: a solution of all-purpose or heavy-duty cleaner (or even plain old hand dishwashing detergent and water) in a spray bottle; a soft white nylon scrub sponge; and a dry cleaning cloth (see page 50) to polish the surface dry right afterward. For those stubborn, dried-on, cooked-on spots, spray and let the solution sit awhile to soften them. Remove and soak any parts that can be detached—shelves, drawers, drip pans, covers, and grills. If you want an appliance exterior to really shine, use glass cleaner to polish it.

To clean under and behind appliances, just use a radiator brush or vacuum dust brush—but unplug any appliance before you start poking around in back of it (so you'll be sure to live to enjoy how clean it is).

Stove and Oven

Spend more time soaking, and you'll spend less time scrubbing. On a conventional-style stovetop, remove the burner pans and any other parts you can, and dump them in hot, soapy water while you clean the rest of the unit. After a good long soaking, you can use a white nylon scrub sponge as needed to help remove the baked-on crud. Spray and wipe the top, back, and sides of the stove. If you have a solid-element cooktop, consult your owner's manual for cleaning instructions. Do the same if you have a glass or ceramic solid-surface cooktop; some of these are downright delicate and can even be scratched by a dirty sponge!

If you come across a hardened spot or spill that doesn't come off an ordinary stovetop easily after the spray-and-sit-awhile treatment or even a work-over with a white nylon sponge, scrub it gently with a plastic or stainless Chore Boy–type scrubber (keep the surface wet while you scrub). Rinse the pad well in hot water afterward, or grease and grime will harden in it.

De-Slob Your Knobs!

Knobs—yes, knobs and dials on stoves—are undoubtedly some of the dirtiest things in the house and are rarely, if ever, cleaned. They really get bad because they're often grooved for easy grip and often have other little ridges and crevices that catch and hold the crud. Most knobs and dials slip right off or only need a simple screw loosened so they can be removed. Toss them into a dishpan (do *them right away so you don't forget about them) and give them the "old toothbrush" (scrubbing) treatment if necessary. Then clean those greasy spots under the knobs before you put them back.*

All of us who still have the old-style ovens clean them the same way, and it's always a tough job. Don't forget to wear rubber gloves, and make sure there's plenty of ventilation—oven cleaner is nasty stuff (for nasty work).

You might want to put a drop cloth or old blanket on the floor in front of the oven when you clean it. Newspaper too often just acts a "strainer" for any spills, which end up "eating" your floor. Apply oven cleaner, and wait . . . and then wait some more. (I'm a "wait-over-nighter," myself.) This is the most important step; the chemical needs time to loosen and dissolve all those drips and spatters and stone-hard lumps. When you've tested for the fourth time and the stuff finally seems to be coming off, wipe off the bulk of the now-brown, murky cleaner with paper towels that you can just throw away. By now you should almost be able to see the actual surface of the oven. Reapply cleaner to any black patches that remain, and let it work through them. Don't scrub—just keep applying oven cleaner as long as you need to and let the chemical do the work for you. Simply wipe away the dissolved mess after each application.

When you're done, be sure to remove all traces of oven cleaner with a damp cloth so your next roast won't reek of chemicals.

Stove Hood and Exhaust Vent

Grease-laden exhaust vents and stove hoods can cause fires, so don't neglect them. Check the manufacturer's instructions if available. You can usually take off the grill, remove the filter, and unplug the unit. Soak the aluminum mesh grease filter in hot dishwashing detergent solution (stubborn deposits might require a strong degreaser solution), or wash it alone in the dishwasher. Rinse in hot water. While the grease filter soaks, use paper towels to wipe off the worst of the sticky, fuzzy grease inside and outside the hood and on the fan blades. Then use a cloth or, if necessary, a white nylon scrub sponge dampened with heavy-duty cleaner or degreaser solution. Deeper cleaning might mean removing the motor and fan assembly; never immerse these parts or spray anything on them or allow water to drip inside. But do wipe off the fan blades and remove the grease and lint from the motor housing. Dry everything, replace the filter, and reassemble.

Refrigerator and Freezer

If you wipe up leaks and spills as soon as they happen and do a quick shelf once-over every week or so with a sponge dipped in clean dishwater, you may be able to avoid the all-out, all-over-the-floor cleaning routine. **Regular reconnaissance in there will also keep your hard-earned food dollars and carefully saved leftovers from being wasted.** An open box of baking soda in the fridge will help keep odor away, and three tablespoons of baking soda mixed with a quart of water makes a good deodorizing solution for an overall wipe down. Gentle all-purpose cleaner is fine, too. Let the solution soften hardened-on food; don't scrub except with a white nylon scrub sponge. Wipe dry with a cleaning cloth. Wash all removable parts in the sink and thoroughly dry them before you put them back.

Chapter Thirteen

Shorter Visits to the Bathroom

The restroom in the commercial building was a sight to behold. A line of sinks stretched to infinity, and the toilet stalls looked like the starting gate at Santa Anita. Although 250 people used this particular restroom, it just radiated cleanliness. The chrome glistened, and the porcelain of the sinks and toilets sparkled germ-free—and the pro cleaner who cleaned it only spent an hour per day to keep it that way. If you use the same method he did, you should be able to keep your home bathroom in that same immaculate condition by cleaning it for just a few minutes a day!

Clean Your Bathroom in 3½ Minutes

Sound impossible? Not if you put some professional techniques to work. The professional approach to cleaning your bathroom is simple and will save you time—the secret, of course, is to spend a few minutes each day keeping it clean rather than executing a big once-a-week clean-and-scrub siege. The preventive approach here—maintaining your bathroom regularly and efficiently—is smart.

Again, tools and supplies are important. You'll have to bite your lip and disregard most of the old standbys such as abrasive cleansers, deodorant sprays, perfumed blocks, wonder wicks, and blue bowl seltzers. The following is a regular cleaning program that eliminates the need for these.

Essential Supplies

To avoid wasted time, damage to fixtures, and poor results, go to the local janitorial-supply store and purchase scented or unscented disinfectant cleaner concentrate—it's what hospitals use. Get a quaternary cleaner; its active ingredient is ammonium chloride. Avoid the phenol-based cleaners—they're too toxic for home use. Diluted according to the directions on the bottle and used correctly, a quaternary cleaner will clean quickly and efficiently, and eradicate or inhibit bacterial growth. This will eliminate not only smells but also the need for expensive perfumed preparations.

Most of us pros use this kind of disinfectant cleaner (nicknamed a "quat"), but if you clean *often* enough, most cleaners will sanitize pretty well. So you could use pine cleaner or (if you live in a hard-water area) phosphoric acid cleaner, too. The secret is regularity—not letting soap scum, dirt, and mineral deposits build up to stone hardness and thickness.

For daily bathroom maintenance use germicidal or disinfectant cleaner diluted from concentrate. Dilute according to directions into a plastic spray bottle. When spraying disinfectant cleaner in a confined area like the bathroom, adjust the nozzle so the droplets will fall when you spray. If the mist is too fine, you'll inhale particles and irritate your throat.

While at the janitorial-supply store, pick up a plastic spray bottle that can be left in the bathroom (get more than one if you have more than one bathroom). Be sure you store the bottle out of the reach of children. Once the spray bottle is filled with the water and disinfectant cleaner in the correct proportion, the only other tools you need are a cleaning cloth and a white nylon scrub sponge for dislodging any persistent residue.

Your daily bathroom-cleaning routine should be something like this: Spray and wipe the mirror with glass cleaner if it's spotted. If not, leave it alone. Next, spray the hardware, sink, and countertops with disinfectant cleaner (spray ahead so the cleaner will soften and break down soil); wipe and buff the surfaces dry with a cleaning cloth. They will sparkle. Do shower stalls and tubs next. Do the toilet last (see pages 192-193).

Once the upper fixtures are clean, spray the floor and, with the already-damp cleaning cloth, wipe it up. This method is a lot faster and better than mixing up mop water and fumbling around with a mop in a 15- or 20-square-foot area.

Spray the mirror, fixtures, sink, and countertops. Wipe and buff dry. Next do the shower stall and tub. Then the toilet (base last!) and floor. Remember that odors are caused by bacteria. A clean bathroom won't need deodorant.

The Benefits of Preventive Maintenance

It takes only minutes to clean a bathroom the spray-disinfectant way, and if you leave a spray bottle and cloth in the room, you can get your bathroom spotless while you wait for Junior to go potty or for the sink to fill up. The system works only if you clean the bathroom regularly, however. It will keep hard-water deposits, soap scum, toilet bowl lines, and other soils from building up and cementing on. The basic reason you needed abrasive cleansers and acids to clean the bathroom in the past was that buildup accumulated to the point of no return and had to be chiseled off instead of wiped off.

Don't use powdered cleansers and steel wool to grind soil off surfaces. In most of the many thousands of houses I've cleaned in my career, the sinks, tubs, and shower units—porcelain, fiberglass, or plastic—have had damage from improper use of acids, cleansers, and abrasive pads. The grinding abrasion that removes spots and stains also removes chrome and porcelain and damages fiberglass. This is a great reason to use the disinfectant cleaner/spray bottle system from the start. Your chrome, plastic, fiberglass, marble, and porcelain will remain bright and sound.

If you have damaged fixtures, you'll have difficulty no matter what you use, because porous surfaces collect gunk quickly and clean up slowly. Many of these surfaces—especially the shower area—will benefit from a coat of paste wax, which helps repel the scum and hard-water buildup. (Just don't wax the shower *floor*!)

A Squeegee in the Shower Is Worth a Truckload of "De-Limer"

You can minimize the problem of shower buildup by simply hanging a fourteen-inch squeegee in the shower. It takes only fifteen seconds for the user to squeegee the wall dry and clean after a shower. If you let hard water dry on your bathroom surfaces over and over again, the built-up minerals will be very difficult to remove.

It's not a bad idea to also wipe down the shower chrome (faucets, etc.) while it's still wet. Use your bath towel to dry it after you dry yourself, and you'll leave it nice and shiny and prevent mineral deposit buildup!

What if you already have hard-water buildup on your walls and fixtures? A professional-strength phosphoric acid "de-scaler" (for home use you don't want anything stronger than 9 percent) will dissolve hard-water buildup faster and better than supermarket de-limers.

For old, stubborn soap scum, try the method just outlined first. Often the hard-water deposits on a surface create little "shelves" of mineral that hold scum.

If that doesn't work, use a degreaser or soap-scum remover from a janitorial-supply store, or a product such as Showers-n-Stuff, which is designed to remove soap scum as well as hard-water deposits.

Be careful with those things the hint-and-tip books tell you to soak in tubs and sinks overnight—such as oven grills, blinds, crusted camping gear, tools, etc. Extended exposure to some normally harmless cleaners can pit your fixtures.

Keep your drain running free by pulling out the stopper every month or so and cleaning the collected hair off it (encouraging hair care to be practiced elsewhere than over the sink can prevent this). Boiling-hot water poured down a drain periodically ought to handle any soap scum buildup that might slow down drainage.

> When a drop of hard or soapy water lands on a surface and dries, the minerals and other residue dissolved in it collect at the base of the drop when it evaporates. Every time the surface gets wet, new drops add to the accumulation—and this will keep building up into a hard, solid deposit. That's why it's smart to clean regularly (especially showers and windows) and not give buildup a chance to happen.

Cleaning Toilets

Briskly scrubbing inside a toilet bowl with a bowl brush for a few seconds each day will retard buildup and remove discoloration and lines. Contrary to popular belief, it's the outside of the toilet that's the most unsanitary. When you do your daily spray-cleaning of the bathroom with disinfectant cleaner, spray and wipe the entire outside of the toilet from top to bottom. Be sure to do the base of the toilet last. This will prevent you from transporting the worst germ concentration to the faucet handles. Every couple of weeks, pour a little disinfectant into the bowl, swish the water around, and let it sit awhile. Remember, it's the outside of the toilet—under the seat and around the rim—that's germiest and will begin to smell if not cleaned frequently. The cold water that enters the bowl with every flush discourages bacterial growth there.

Still finding hair clinging to the bathroom toilet, sink, and walls after cleaning? Before you start cleaning, wet a dab of toilet paper and swipe up all the fugitive hair.

If you need to remove old buildup in the toilet, do it right. Don't pour steaming acid into the water-filled bowl and slosh it around. Dilution with water neutralizes the power of any

Do force the water out of the bowl with a swab or bowl brush.

Soak the swab with bowl cleaner, lightly coat the bowl, and flush to rinse.

bowl cleaner. Instead, a couple of times a year, grab a swab (see the equipment chart in Chapter 5) and push it quickly up and down in the bowl toward the "throat" of the toilet. All the water will vanish. Then moisten the swab with bowl cleaner and coat the inside of the toilet bowl. Let the cleaner sit on there a few minutes, then flush to rinse. Reapply, let sit, and rinse again as necessary until all the deposits are gone.

If a ring remains, don't get excited and acid-bath the whole unit. The ring is the result of hard-water deposit that's left as water in the toilet evaporates. A pumice stone will remove almost any ring (be sure the surface is wet when using it or it will scratch).

Remember to swab the bowl regularly to prevent buildup. And don't stake your hopes on "miracle" toilet cleaners that promise to make the job fun and easy—there's no such thing out there yet. The "automatic bowl cleaners" that go in the flush tank are a help in keeping things sanitary, but they aren't a substitute for periodic deep cleaning. Even if you can't see the ring, it's still there—you just can't see it because it's bleached white. You still need to go over the bowl with a bowl swab now and then to keep it from building up.

Basic Bowl Cleaner Technique

For daily maintenance, scrub briskly inside the bowl with a bowl brush. You only need to use acid bowl cleaner every so often.

When you do:
- Don't pour bowl cleaner into the water.
- Do force the water out of the bowl with a swab or bowl brush.
- Soak the swab with bowl cleaner, lightly coat the bowl—and flush to rinse.

How to Get Rid of Bathroom Mildew

When warm, humid weather and spores of mold team up, those little black spots of mildew can grow on everything, including drawers, closets, books, and shoes. Aside from the basement, mildew's favorite home is the bathroom.

The best way to get rid of mildew is to prevent it. See Chapter 8 for household-wide tips for preventing mildew.

Using disinfectant in the bathroom and shower area discourages mildew growth there. Chlorine bleach kills mildew, but won't prevent it from returning; you can only do that by altering conditions favorable for growth. Drying out a bathroom that several people bathe and shower in every day is difficult, so all you can really do is keep cleaning with disinfectant—and hitting mildewed grout with a weak chlorine bleach solution (one part bleach to five parts cool water)—as long as the tile isn't made of plastic and you're careful not to get the bleach on anything that is.

Doorknobs and Telephones

If people were asked to list the most unsanitary objects in the home most of them would remember the toilet but forget doorknobs. It wouldn't hurt, while armed with a spray bottle of disinfectant cleaner, to go through the house and spray and wipe all the doorknobs occasionally (and the light switches, chair backs, and telephone receivers). When things like cleaning light switches or telephones, spray the cleaner onto a cloth and use it to wipe.

Chapter Fourteen
Success in High Places

One of my customers had a husband full of ambition and desire to clean, but he was terrified of high places. She would hire me to wash all the high areas, saving the low stuff for him. One year, while cleaning his low section, he was on a plank just a foot off the floor when he was seized by his phobia. He lay down on the plank, dug his whitened fingertips into the wood, and froze. His wife, unable to talk him down from that dizzying height, ended up calling the fire department (siren and all!). They finally dislodged the husband's death grip on the plank and got him to floor level safely, but he was never sound enough emotionally to assist in cleaning again.

Easy Access, Easy Cleaning

Be sure to adjust or limit the reaching of tall areas to fit your resources, age, and nerves (and your helpers' bravery!). But don't be buffaloed by hard-to-reach areas. The time it takes to get ready and going is the bane of cleaning in high places. "Once I got up there, it only took ten minutes" is what we often hear (or say). Easy access contributes greatly to success in such cleaning, yet the shaky old ladder and unsteady stepstool are about the extent of most homes' scaffolding. More energy, time, and emotion are used going up and down the ladder or stool than actually doing the job. And all of our effort, worry, tool procurement, and arrangement seem to be focused on the few minutes we'll actually perform the job, instead of trying to speed up the business of getting in position to start it.

The equipment needed to reach the work has to be light enough to be manageable, and small enough to fit in tight areas and keep from scratching walls and woodwork. It must be *sturdy* and *safe* enough to ensure no falls. The following is the basic equipment that more than fifty years of housecleaning have taught me to use.

To reach high cabinets, curtain rods, etc., people usually climb on the harmless-looking kitchen stool or bench. These have a narrow base and a deceptively sturdy top. But they're too unbalanced and risky to use as a standing or cleaning tool, as is the equally unsafe kitchen chair.

A Good Ladder

A plain old common ladder is one of your best all-around tools. It's versatile, manageable, and safe . . . if you choose the right model. For household use, the perfect stepladder height is 5 feet. Four-foot ladders are too short to work on 8-foot ceilings; a 6-foot ladder is too high, and it nicks up the house when you carry it around. Instead of buying several creaky wooden ladders during your lifetime, buy a 5-foot heavy-duty commercial aluminum ladder. You'll never regret it. It's stronger and sturdier, and will probably outlast you—even counting the ten years it may add to your life. It can be used outside on rough terrain, and neither bad weather nor dry storage will hurt it.

A 5-foot ladder is just right for household cleaning

For higher reaches, every household should also have a tall ladder, and the perfect one for this purpose is an 18-foot, two-piece extension ladder. It will collapse to 10 feet for storage and lengthen out safely to 16 feet—enough to get the cat out of the tree, put up the holiday lights, or paint the trim every five years. Aluminum is lighter, but in an extension ladder for home use, fiberglass (these usually have aluminum rungs) is better for electrical protection. Don't paint wooden ladders; paint hides breaks, cracks, and flaws and is slippery when wet. Instead, use boiled linseed oil to maintain wooden ladders. It penetrates the wood and keeps water out and slivers in. A coat every five years will keep a ladder happy. When you oil a ladder, leave it at least overnight before using it again.

Walk the Plank . . . for Safety

The last and most useful tool to help you conquer the unreachable places is a sturdy, ordinary 2 × 12-inch plank, 8 to 10 feet long. Purchase your plank at a lumberyard and make sure it has no loose knots, cracks, or weak areas. Redwood is good because it's light and rot-resistant. (Pine, fir, aspen, or hemlock will also work all right, but they're not nearly as light.) Sand off the corners and rough edges for ease of handling, and it's ready to use. Don't paint or varnish it or it will be slippery when wet. Though it may be scary at first, a plank is safe to work on if you're reasonably awake. You'll soon get used to the slight spongy "give" you'll feel. It is one of the best "under $20" investments you'll ever make.

The idea is to combine two stepladders, an extension ladder, and the plank in a number of ways to reach your working area easily, safely, and without wasted motion. If you need to reach higher areas than can be reached with this combination, rent the necessary equipment, because you'll seldom use it around the house. It is also extremely risky to tie or lay a plank on planters, metal railings, fireplace mantels, or other trim. Most of these were designed to be looked at, not to support 150 pounds or more of plank, cleaning tools, and person. Place ladders and plank on supports where strength is certain.

The plank-and-ladder combination is especially effective in high stairwells. On stair landings and other open areas, you can figure out a combination. It will make you love yourself for your brilliance.

For maximum stability, be sure your plank extends at least a few inches beyond the end of the ladder rungs it's set on.

You're usually only about 2 feet off the floor when you do ceilings from a ladder. In a stairwell, you are higher over the stairs, but with the walls of the narrow landing on both sides of you and with a ladder at both ends, there is little risk of falls.

When an extension ladder is leaned against something, it must be tilted at the proper angle to keep it from slipping down or tumbling over. One foot out from the base of the wall for every 4 feet up is just right. Keep your cleaning solution, tools, paint, and other working materials as close to you as possible by wearing a pocketed apron or by setting your gear on the plank. Ascending or descending a ladder or plank for every dip depletes strength, wastes time, and exposes you more often to potential mishap.

Be sure to adjust or limit the reaching of high areas to fit your age, nerves, and bravery. If you have an overwhelming fear of heights, don't do it—you'll get hurt. If you have no fear of heights, get smart—you can get hurt. If heights make you shake in your boots, find a couple of daredevils and hire them to climb to clean off those flyspecks, change a light bulb, or paint or wash the ceiling. Or trade them a favor for the purpose.

To Clean a Stair Landing

Lean your extension ladder (padded with a towel or dry sponges) against the wall with the base angled into the stairs. Open your stepladder at the top of the stairs. The plank, set across a lower rung of the stepladder and a rung of the extension ladder, puts you in a safe, convenient position to clean or paint the walls. Padding the "wall" end of your plank if it touches the wall will protect the wall.

One trick I've tried without much success is moving a stepladder without moving the buckets or tools off it first. I bat about 60 percent. The other 40 percent has cost me wet carpets, skinned shins, painted faces, and trips back to the starting gate.

To use a ladder safely: Angle one foot from the wall for every 4 feet of height. Never stand on the very top of the ladder, or on the top rung.

A cleaning towel (see Chapter 15) slipped over each of the ladder's upper legs will keep it from marking up your walls. A dry sponge (see Chapter 15) under each leg will prevent it from slipping if the surface the legs rest on is questionable. Tennis shoes on your feet will prevent *you* from slipping, too.

A final word of advice: Put your name on your ladders and planks. When your neighbors spot them, they will be only too happy to try out your new way of reaching high places.

Chapter Fifteen
Simplified Wall and Ceiling Cleaning

I once bid to wash the walls in six large offices, a long hall, lobby, the entrances, and storage areas in a Massey Ferguson tractor dealer's office. Back in the 1960s when a dollar was a dollar, I was the low bid at the price of $275. The rest of my crew was busy on the scheduled day, so I tackled the job alone. Seven hours later, I had it finished and received more than a few compliments on the quality of the job.

On another occasion, I washed all the walls, ceilings, and woodwork in a modern three-bedroom home in less than one day—alone. Now, I'm no more a "super" wall and ceiling cleaner than you are. In fact, I'm certain that many of you could keep up with or beat me on my best day, if you'd use the same approach I did.

Your days of struggling with a bucket of grimy wall-washing solution will end as you finish this chapter, if you follow the simple principles it sets forth. We outlined the basic principle of cleaning—eliminate, saturate, dissolve, remove—in

Chapter 6; here's how that principle applies to the technique and tools of wall cleaning.

The Versatile Dry Sponge

A very useful (and little-known) tool of housecleaning is a rubber sponge called a dry sponge. It works just like a rubber eraser, removing and absorbing dirt. Dry sponges are generally tan 5" × 7" × ½" pads. Never, never use water on them or get them wet—not a drop—or they will become useless for cleaning.

Dry sponges are excellent on wallpaper—much better than "dough" wallpaper cleaners that crumble and stick! On ceiling acoustical tile and on most flat oil- or latex-painted walls, one swipe of a dry sponge will remove the dirt. It won't remove fingerprints or flyspecks or grease—only the film of dirt. In most homes, dry-sponging the ceiling will leave it perfect. I washed behind a dry sponge several times at first, not believing that the sponge could get all the dirt out, but it did—every bit of it! In fact, on many porous walls or painted surfaces where the dirt is embedded deeply, a dry sponge is superior to washing. Even on walls that are smoke-damaged, ten minutes of dry-sponging the room prior to washing will reduce washing time and expense by more than 50 percent.

When dry-sponging, you don't have to stop to dip or rinse. Just get to the surface and swipe in 4-foot lengths (or shorter if your arms are shorter). The sponge will absorb the dirt and begin to get black. A dry sponge has eight good working surfaces, if folded and used correctly. It will hold the dirt as you clean along, but as soon as it reaches its saturation point, turn or refold the sponge and keep going.

A dry sponge won't clean enamel or greasy surfaces, so don't be disappointed when you make a swipe across the kitchen or bathroom wall and nothing dramatic happens.

If you go into the bedroom and make a swipe across the ceiling or outside wall and can't see where you've just been, those surfaces don't need cleaning, and the rest of the walls probably don't either.

The residue that falls from the sponge won't stain or stick and is easily vacuumed up after the job is done. When a dry sponge is black on both sides, throw it away. Washing it doesn't work. Dry sponges cost about $2 and are worth ten times that for the job they do and the time they save.

Once the dry-sponging is out of the way, the remaining areas not cleaned with a dry sponge will have to be washed. You can accomplish this rather simply if you use the right tools and methods.

Your Rag Is Your Worst Enemy

There is no question that the most famous household cleaning tool is the simple little item known as a "rag." You have salvaged rags from ancient sheets, tattered curtains, worn-out jeans, and other fabric scraps. Using a rag to clean is like using a rake to comb your hair. For hundreds of years cloth manufacturers have worked to develop fabrics that repel liquids and stains. They've succeeded, and we have scores of fabrics today that resist moisture—which makes them terrible cleaning tools. Yet we can't seem to resist saving trouser legs, old slips, T-shirts, and a thousand other unsuitable fabrics for cleaning rags. Don't do it!

One thing that makes the professional a much faster and better cleaner than the home cleaner is the fact that home cleaners are hung up on rags. Rags are only good for paint cleanup, stuffing rag dolls, or signaling surrender when the cleaning gets you down. Henceforth, the term "rag" must be banished from your housecleaning vocabulary and from your basket of cleaning tools. The rag in your housecleaning tool bag will be replaced with an item called a "cleaning cloth" (see next section).

The Noble Cleaning Cloth

A cleaning cloth is made from a new or salvaged heavy cotton terry or "Turkish" towel. Be sure to use toweling with high cotton content—ideally 100 percent cotton.

You can make either plain square cloths or the "tube" style we pros favor. Cut an eighteen-by-eighteen-inch piece of toweling. For the plain style, just hem all of the edges and you're done. For the tube style, fold the same size piece in half, and sew the edges of the long side together, leaving it open on both ends like a tube. By folding the tube twice, you have a hand-sized surface of thick, absorbent terry that will efficiently cover every inch of surface it passes over—and even get down into textured walls and floors. It's not like the old bed sheet that just streaks and smears the film around.

How to Make a Cleaning Cloth

1. Cut an 18″ x 18″ square of heavy terry.
2. Fold and stitch together on the long side; hem all of the edges.
3. It will be hollow like a tube.

How to Use It

1. Fold it once.
2. Fold again and it will just fit your hand.
3. By changing sides and turning it inside out, you have sixteen sides to clean with.
4. Soiled cleaning cloths are simply washed and tumble-dried for reuse.

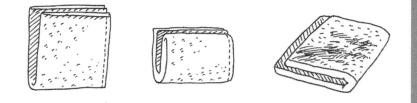

If you fold your cleaning towels correctly and use both sides, you have eight efficient surfaces to use; turn the towel inside out and you have eight more. Sixteen surfaces on one little cleaning cloth!

Terry cleaning cloths will protect your hands from scrapes, cuts, and ripped fingernails, too. You can clean all the walls of a large room using only three cleaning cloths. **Twenty cleaning cloths will clean your entire house and, if washed properly, will last for years.** When you finish and the cleaning cloths are damp and dirty, just throw them into the washer. You don't have to use much detergent, because the towels will be full of the cleaner you've been using. If you wash the towels while they're still wet, they'll come out as clean as they were before you used them (although in time they'll get dingy and battle-scarred, but they'll still be clean—just stained). Be sure to tumble-dry them! If you hang them on a clothesline they'll be stiff as a board and impossible to use the next time.

Your Basic Wall-Cleaning Tools

The dry sponge and cleaning cloth are the main professional tools you need for your wall cleaning, so don't prepare a long list of materials and equipment. The rest of the items you probably already have around the house, so round them up:

- One empty bucket (plastic won't skin up the furniture or sweat like metal does)
- One bucket half full of warm water
- An ordinary cellulose sponge (preferably about 1½ inches thick; make sure the other dimensions fit your hand)
- Some all-purpose cleaner or heavy-duty cleaner if the wall is extra dirty or greasy

You're probably thinking, "Wouldn't a two-compartment bucket be great!" No, it wouldn't. They are, without question, one of the most worthless instruments ever palmed off on a housecleaner. Just try to pour dirty water out of one side and keep clean water in the other—or to carry the thing without any intermingling!

Mix your cleaning solution following the directions on the container. Make sure your cleaning compound is one capable of cutting the dirt you want to remove. Ammonia or all-purpose cleaner will be fine unless you're dealing with an extremely grease-laden kitchen, where using heavy-duty cleaner or a little degreaser added to the solution will make the job much easier. For bathroom walls, you might want to use a disinfectant cleaner. Fill your bucket only half full (if you fill it to the brim it'll be top-heavy and can easily spill).

If you hustle, you should be able to wash a room in thirty minutes, but you'll probably want to allow yourself an hour (maybe more if you anticipate being interrupted).

Cleaning Procedure

You have your ladder or scaffolding in position, and now you're ready to begin my method of wall cleaning. You won't have to cover everything before you start because there will be little or no dripping. Although, if you have a grand piano or piece of expensive antique furniture that a drop or two might hurt, don't take the chance—throw a drop cloth or sheet of light plastic over it. Upholstered furniture can usually be moved out of the way rather than covered. **A drop of cleaning solution won't hurt most things if it's removed immediately, but if it's not cleaned up right away, it may spot or ruin the finish.**

Placing your bucket of solution in the right place is extremely important. It should be where you don't have to climb 30 feet to dip your sponge; *always keep it as close to your working area as possible.* (Spilling solution was a major problem in my beginning housecleaning days. I finally learned to set the bucket next to me near the wall—not in back of me, nor on a table, nor in the middle of the floor.) Be sure to set your bucket in a visible spot. The most common spillage problems involve tripping over buckets or knocking them over while moving a piece of furniture. If you do spill a bucket of solution on carpet, run for the wet-dry vacuum and get out all the moisture you can. Then rinse with clear water to get the ammonia (or other cleaning agent) out.

Take your sponge now and dip it about ½-inch into the solution (not all the way in). This will give you plenty of solution to wet the wall or ceiling, yet leave the rest of the sponge dry enough to absorb any water that otherwise would splash into your eyes or run down your arms.

I know all the books say to start at the bottom of the wall and work up, because if you dribble on the lower unwashed wall from the top, it might stain; this is an old wives' tale.

Anyone who tells you that doesn't know how to wash walls. In extreme cases with, say, fifty-year-old paints or spectacularly dirty walls, it might be wise, but it's discouraging to start at the bottom, get it clean, then go on to the top and dribble on the clean wall.

How large an area you work on at one time depends, of course, on:

1. Your reach
2. How soiled the surface is
3. How fast the solution will dry on the surface

A 3 × 3-foot section is just about right for the average person. Quickly cover the section with the solution on the sponge. Don't press hard or water will spurt out and drip on the carpet and your head. Gently spread the liquid on the surface. By the time you get to the end of the section, the initial application of solution will have worked the dirt loose. Now go back to the starting point and again go over the area gently. Don't squeeze the sponge! By now, the chemicals in your cleaning solution have loosened the dirt, and it will come off and soak into the sponge. In the other hand, folded to perfection, is your cleaning cloth. Use it now to quickly wipe and buff the area before it dries. No rinsing is necessary. The wiping will not only remove the remaining cleaner and dirt, but it will also polish off the scum that so often streaks washed walls.

Now the critical procedure: Hold the sponge over the empty bucket and *squeeze,* don't wring. When you squeeze the sponge, the dirty solution will go into the empty bucket, leaving the sponge damp and clean. Again, dip the sponge into the bucket of cleaning solution about ½-inch and repeat the process until the room is bright and clean.

How to Clean a Wall

1. First you need a bucket half filled with warm ammonia or all-purpose cleaner solution, an empty bucket, a sponge, and a cleaning cloth.

2. Dip the sponge about ½-inch into the solution.

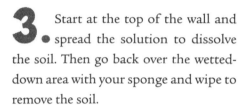

3. Start at the top of the wall and spread the solution to dissolve the soil. Then go back over the wetted-down area with your sponge and wipe to remove the soil.

4. Wipe the sponged area with a folded cleaning cloth.

5. Squeeze (don't twist!) the dirty sponge into the empty bucket. Then dip the sponge into the clean solution again and repeat.

6. When you finish, the bucket that started out empty will be full of dirty water.

Your cleaning solution will stay crystal clean—the chemical will always be working full strength. You'll notice that the empty bucket is beginning to fill with filthy black gunk, while the sponge that you dip into the cleaning solution each time is a squeezed-out hungry sponge (not a sponge full of dirty cleaner), so the dirt never touches your cleaning solution. This means that every drop going on each new section of wall is powerful, unpolluted cleaning solution that will do most of the work. The old method you once used—scrubbing, dipping your sponge in the solution, wringing it, and scrubbing again—always left your cleaning water murky and filthy and thus without full cleaning power. It would streak the walls and have to be changed every fifteen minutes, taking up a lot of time and wasting a lot of cleaning solution. With the two-bucket method you don't spend time scrubbing, just applying and removing. And the cleaning cloth dries and polishes walls three times as well as the old rags you once used. Some other things to remember:

- Don't be surprised that "outside walls" (the inside surfaces of exterior walls) will be dirtier than inside or "partition" walls.
- If you can't see where you're going when you wash, forget it—it doesn't need washing!
- Do dump the dirty water in the toilet regularly (after each room), because you'll have a tough cleanup problem if it spills.

Two-Bucket Benefits

Besides doing a much faster and better job, the two-bucket wall-cleaning technique has two more great "Life After Housework" savers:

1. You'll never dump and refill another bucket of solution. One bucket of water and fifty cents worth of solution will do all the walls in your house!
2. The dirty water . . . you will love it. In fact you will have a special relationship to it. Before, all your evidence of toil and accomplishment went down the drain—now you have it for show.

Enameled Walls

When cleaning enamel-painted halls, kitchens, or bathrooms, use the same procedure, with one simple adjustment: Keep the drying towels cleaner and drier, because enamel needs more polishing with a drier buffing cloth than flat paint. Wipe marks won't show on flat paints, but they will show even on perfectly clean enamel. Those circular wipe marks that you can't see when you finish (but that you can see later in certain light) are caused by rags; rags won't buff dry your walls.

I was called back on many jobs during my first year of cleaning to remove streaks that weren't there when I left. Since the day many years ago now when I began to use terry cleaning cloths I haven't been called back for a single case of "enamel streak."

P.S. Plain sheetrock can't be washed. It's just paper over gypsum with joints made of tape plus a spackling-type compound—it'll just turn to putty if it's wet. Paint it with two coats of enamel and next time you'll be able to wash it.

How to Clean . . .

- **Paneling:** Use the same procedure as for painted walls. On wooden paneling, use oil soap solution, keep the sponge nearly dry, and then, buffing with the grain, dry completely with a cleaning cloth.

- **Wallpaper:** Use a dry sponge and clean with the flow of the design.
- **Vinyl wall covering:** Use the cleaner recommended by the manufacturer, keeping the sponge nearly dry. Use no harsh or abrasive cleaners. Then dry thoroughly with a cleaning cloth.
- **Textured wall coverings:** Any textured wall covering will have dust and dirt resting in the thousands of little pockets of the design, which will spread out all over when the wall is wet or rubbed. Vacuum walls like these first before wet- or dry-cleaning.

What to Do about Wall Spots

Don't try to clean spots or marks before you wash down the whole wall—they might come off with the first washing. Let the solution do the work! If the spots don't come off when you wash them, just leave them until you finish.

Then come back and try to remove them. Most wall marks can be removed by simply finding a cleaning agent with the same base as the spot. On a tar spot, for example, you can scrub and rub with high-powered cleaners, sweat and swear, and still not get the spot out. A little paint thinner (which has a solvent base) will remove it in three seconds without hurting the wall. Use your head, not your hands, whenever possible, and you won't scour off the paint.

Toothpaste, peanut butter, or abrasive cleansers will get many marks off, but they will also take off the paint or at least make a too-visible spot on the wall. If you must scrub to remove a spot, wet a cleaning cloth with your wall-cleaning solution and try that, or a white nylon scrub sponge wetted with the solution.

If all else fails, wall marks can be coated with a stain-blocking primer such as KILZ and then repainted.

Cleaning Woodwork

You can wash the woodwork or baseboards while doing the walls, but it's not the best option because woodwork is usually covered with lint, hair, dead bugs, etc., which will get into your sponge and be difficult to get out. Before you start washing the room, use a damp paper towel to wipe the baseboards and door frames and the like and pick up all of the residue, then just dispose of it. Use a damp cleaning cloth to finish up, if need be, streak- and lint-free. You can also vacuum the woodwork well before wiping it down.

How to Clean Paneling

Remember that raw wood must be coated with a finish so that moisture won't penetrate it. Then you'll be cleaning the finish, not the wood itself—it's faster, and much easier on the wood and you!

Unfinished wood may look "warm and homey," but if anything like markers or grease gets to it, the stain will sink into the surface and be very difficult or impossible to remove. A satin-finish polyurethane or varnish finish will dry to a low sheen and preserve the natural look of the wood. (Follow the instructions on the can, remember to stir well, and keep your work area as dust-free as you can.)

On wood paneling with a sealed surface, or on vinyl paneling (much "imitation wood" paneling is actually vinyl, or vinyl-coated composition board), use only a mild oil soap or neutral all-purpose cleaner solution, and apply it sparingly with a sponge. I use an oil soap called Wood Wash that I had a chemical company formulate for me; you could also use one of the vegetable oil soaps on the market such as Murphy. Then, going with the grain so that streaks will not be noticeable, dry-buff with a cleaning cloth. A clean, dry surface on a paneled wall is much better than covering the paneling with

"El Gunko" panel polish or cleaners that leave a sticky surface or collect and hold handprints and every passing particle of dirt and dust. The oil soap cleans the wood surface and leaves a nice shine.

Cleaning Ceilings

Ceilings are always tough, even the easier-to-clean types (like enamel) with no texture or special finish of any kind.

You don't have to wash the ceiling every time you wash the walls (ceiling-washing is hard work, even for experienced experts). Ceilings only need cleaning about one-third as often as walls; unless you have a ceiling heat vent or exhaust fan, and then you can just clean the area around it and feather the cleaning line. Except where they are exposed to fireplace fumes and cigarette smoke, ceilings just don't get the abuse that walls do. They don't have the fingerprints, crayon marks, and everyday spatters, so they can go several years between cleanings. Kitchen ceilings, which often get airborne grease from cooking, may be the exception.

For fairly smooth ceilings with washable paint (gloss or semigloss enamel), use the same two-bucket technique described for wall washing. If the ceiling is greasy or smoke-coated, use heavy-duty cleaner or degreaser solution rather than all-purpose cleaner.

Ceilings made of sealed wood should be cleaned the same as sealed wood paneling.

Watch Where You Set It!

In the rush and push of a big cleaning project, we've all set a sponge or cloth down, then gone off and forgotten it. After ruining a grand piano and a wooden floor or two, I've learned never to set a wet tool anywhere but back in the bucket or cleaning caddy.

Most flat-painted ceilings can be cleaned quite well by wiping with a dry sponge. Should a few flyspecks remain, dip a cotton swab in white shoe polish or matching paint to mask them. Flat paints are not very washable, no matter what the label says. You almost always leave streaks and lap lines when washing them. It's usually faster and easier to just roll on another coat of paint, especially if you're faced with heavy smoke or water stains, hanging lamp scars, etc.

When you clean the ceiling, first take down any light-fixture diffusers or globes; pour cleaning solution on them, and let them soak in the sink while you clean the ceiling. After you finish the room, use a cleaning cloth to wipe the loosened film and dirt from the parts soaking in the sink. Rinse with hot water, dry, and put them back up immediately.

Textured Ceilings

Builders leave textured ceilings unpainted in a new home. When the ceiling needs cleaning five to seven years later, it can't be washed because the texture (which is a water-based compound) will dissolve when water touches it. If you roll on one coat of latex paint when the ceiling is new, it will "fill" the texture and leave the ceiling looking fantastic. But five years later when you try to wash it, the moisture gets to the compound (which turns brown when wet) and you have a streak. So always paint two coats on an unpainted ceiling and it will be sealed enough to clean.

If a ceiling has deep texturing, get a 4-foot board first and drag it across the surface to knock off all of those sharp little points that prick fingers and chew up sponges. This won't hurt the looks of the ceiling. You can use coarse sandpaper to do the same thing. Then use an extra fluffy roller to apply two coats of good-quality satin enamel. After this dries you can apply the same solution used for washing walls to the ceiling with sponge or brush, wiping away the loosened dirt, and drying the surface with a cleaning cloth.

Acoustical Tile Ceilings

Acoustical ceilings generally won't show dirt until it's too late to clean them. Clean them annually with a dry sponge; it will only take a few minutes. A badly dirtied acoustical ceiling can be resprayed with an acoustic finish or cleaned by the bleaching or oxidation process. You could do this yourself with supplies from a janitorial-supply store, but it's safer to have a professional do it for you. If you paint an acoustical ceiling, you'll ruin the looks and the acoustics.

If you have either "cottage cheese" or those sparkly ceilings, your cleaning choices are limited. You can try vacuuming them with the dust brush of a vacuum, or dry-sponging them. Fortunately these types of ceilings are going out of style.

Washing Closets

You can probably get by with washing the inside of the closets once every ten or fifteen years or so; most closets are closed, so they don't get dirty. Closets generally take longer than the whole room (because you have to empty out all that clutter first, and you are working in such a confined space), and besides, nobody ever sees them anyway. But when you paint your closets, use a hard-finish, light-colored enamel so they'll be easy to clean whenever you do wash them.

Don't Forget the Doors

Our doors get much more use than any other part of the house, yet we spend very little time keeping them clean and looking sharp. Doors are so taken for granted we seldom appreciate their contribution to a neat, attractive house.

When I finished a cleaning marathon on our house one day, the house still looked unfinished for some reason. When I looked around, the floor glistened, the walls were clean, and there was no dust anywhere—but the *doors* had marks all over them. Marks from hands, scratches from carrying suitcases through, the black marks from kicks, mop, and vacuum bumps, etc.

Most of our doors were natural wood with a clear finish, and some were painted. I cleaned the painted doors with a white nylon scrub sponge and all-purpose cleaner. If marks and nicks were still showing or the doors were dull, I simply repainted them. The natural wood doors, I scrubbed with an ammonia solution and white nylon scrub sponge. I cleaned with the grain of the wood and rinsed the cleaner off with a damp cloth. They were now clean, but a little dull. I made sure they were dry and with some extrafine sandpaper, I again went over the door, lightly, with the grain. The sanding removed lint, dust, and hairs that got in the previous coat of finish. I took a cloth dampened with mineral spirits (tack cloths work well, too) and wiped the doors to get off every speck of lint and dust. (By the way, I left the doors on while doing all this and put cardboard under them to protect the rugs and floor.)

Doorknob Dodging

It took twenty years of professional painting for me to finally learn that loosening the two screws on the doorknob so I could paint around it sure beats trying to mask it or sash it with a brush.

I then applied a coat of low-gloss varnish (you could also use a polyurethane finish) to each door (even on the tops), rolling it on so it was evenly distributed, and then brushing with the grain to prevent runs and misses. Then I let them dry.

You won't believe the difference a treatment like this will make in your doors' appearance and the ease of keeping them clean in the future! Pick a day when the house is quiet—when signs and warnings about keeping out of varnish aren't needed. Do the doors on a dry summer day and they'll dry quickly; on a rainy day it can take much longer for them to dry. As soon as your bedroom door is dry enough to close, take a rest. You deserve it for all the time and money you have saved.

Remember—when there's a wall, there's a way!

Chapter Sixteen

If You Have a Dirty House and Just a Few Minutes . . .

At my cleaning seminars and conventions, when I speak on time management, I always ask the audience (whose ages range from twenty-five to ninety-five): "How many of you notice, as you grow older, that you find more time?"

Even in the largest groups, not one hand goes up; not even retired people report that they suddenly have "more time." My parents ran a large ranch almost alone, yet they still seemed to have time when they were younger to go fishing and visit neighbors. After they retired, I couldn't believe how busy they were. I almost needed an appointment to see them. Now my own family is grown, too, but with more than a dozen grandkids and several businesses, I have to beg and pry and hustle to do half the things necessary to live a satisfied life. You know what I mean; it's happened to you. We just don't have the time to get our slice of life and still do justice to our home and its contents.

This chapter outlines a professional strategy for cleaning the whole house quickly. It's a way out for when you have "the house to clean": the whole house—living room, bedrooms, kids' rooms, kitchen and, yes (shudder), even the garage.

First: Trash and Police

Armed with a box or the biggest of all garbage containers, first quickly scout your entire home and dump the trash and garbage—get rid of what's in the wastebaskets as well as what's just lying around (old newspapers, soda cans, petrified pizza crusts, etc.).

As for the clothes, cups, pillows, and all those other things people were "too tired to put back where they belong"—the most loving people leave that stuff behind in the nicest homes in the world. To police the place, carry a plastic laundry basket with you and toss in all the dropped socks and jackets, and all the stray towels and shoes. That way, you can pick up the whole place really quickly, and when you get to the laundry or the utility room it only takes a couple of minutes to toss the dirty clothes in the hamper and quickly assemble everything else—dishes, books, magazines, mail, earrings, hats, duffel bags, tools, school papers, toys, etc.—together with its kind for later dispersal. Dump any questionable stuff into a box that you designate "Lost and Found."

If you do these two things first, you won't believe how much cleaning is already done when you hit the individual areas. You'll be amazed how fast you did all this—in maybe ten or fifteen minutes, especially if you do both jobs on the run. **Once you get your system down, this whole-house overhaul can all be done in a couple of hours or less.** Soon you'll be racing the clock instead of watching it. A streamlined system like this may also eventually tempt some of the other household residents who haven't turned much of a hand to help in the past.

Bedroom

Take care of your bedroom first. Psychologically, it's the easiest to clean, and offers the most instant gratification. And it'll be pretty clean to start with now that the litter and clutter is gone. Only a few things remain. With all your equipment in your cleaning caddy and a lambswool duster in hand, start from the right and work to the left:

1. *Make the bed.* You should have made it when you got out, but if you didn't, make two trips, one stop on each side. First go to the most restless sleeper's side, straighten out all the layers, and pull them into place (pull everything over about a foot farther than you need to on that side). Then go to the other side, straighten, and when you pull the missing foot of cover back from the other side it will tighten the covers to perfection. Once you work up some speed, a bed should take between one and two minutes to make. If you use a comforter instead of a bedspread, you're looking at thirty seconds. Do the bed first so stuff doesn't fall into it as you dust.

2. *Dust.* Start with the high dusting. Don't take time to look and see if there are cobwebs; just take a second to hit those corners. Catch the wall lightly as you go by because dust hangs on the wall and, by keeping it down, you'll keep wall washing to a minimum. Get the light fixtures, door frames, and tops of the doors and drapes. As you move down off the high dusting, hit the lamps on the dressers, the tops of mirrors, and any furniture. Just dust around any doilies or dresser scarves. Then do the fronts and sides of the furniture and work from right to left around the room. (If you feel brave, step in the closet for a second and hit the dust on the shoulders of your hanging clothes.) Don't forget the front of the TV if you have one in there. As you dust down the wall to the floor, make

sure you remove any dust buildup on furniture legs, and the like, and the baseboards.

3. *Straighten up any items on the nightstand and dresser,* and in the headboard if it has shelves.

4. *Spray some glass cleaner on a cleaning cloth and hit the mirrors,* and then with all-purpose cleaner do any handprints on the walls, door frames, and dresser tops (they get pretty grungy from all those set-down coffee cups and all that pocket residue).

5. *Now bring in the vacuum and do the vacuuming*—start at the farthest corner of the room and work your way out. In quick routine cleaning like this, hit the traffic lanes and as far under the bed as you can reasonably reach. But keep that thing moving. As you back your way out of the room, park the vacuum just outside the door. (And yes, clean the doorknob as you go.)

That was your bedroom, and you should have been able to do it in 7½ to 11 minutes, max. Now on to the guest room, or, heaven forbid, the kids' room—but it does have to be done.

Kids' Room

This is often, to put it mildly, a cleaning challenge.

1. First, remove any poten-
tially damaging stuff that might spill, grow mushrooms, or injure carpeting, furniture, or innocent bystanders.

2. Grab that thing that's old and worn and ugly and always in the way and stuff it in a closet, out of sight.

3. As for litter, you trashed and dumped a lot on the initial run-though, so there'll be surprisingly little left. If you clean their room entirely, you'll teach kids that they're

not responsible for their own messes, so sweep and pile the rest in the center and leave a note. My daughter gets great results from her kids with "No Pizza Hut until all this is gone."

4. Dust any horizontal surfaces visible beneath the clutter, and spot-clean the black marks and handprints (the kids will never see them).

5. Leave the vacuuming for them, too. Vacuum handles fit any size hand, and what kid isn't just itching for a chance to drive something? If they can plug in a Nintendo, a vacuum is a cinch.

The time you spend in the kids' room will depend on how determined a delegator you are. If you get your kids to pitch in, you'll be out of there in five or six minutes. Otherwise, you'll probably spend ten to twelve minutes in the junior jungle.

Halls and Entryways

Halls are fast and easy; they're kind of the rapids of the home: Little accumulates or stays there in the swift current.

1. *Dusting is probably the biggest issue in a hall.* All those bodies moving through distribute dust onto wall hangings, door frames, and light fixtures. Hit the hallway running with your lambswool duster. The lighting in a hallway isn't always the greatest but you should be able to catch the cobwebs. Dust well. Get those corners, chandeliers, and the tops and fronts of wall hangings and furniture. Don't forget the baseboard.

2. *Spot-clean next.* Narrow halls (which means most of them) get fingerprints, bumps, grazes, and lean marks. Armed with your spray bottle of all-purpose cleaner and cloth, touch them up. Get them as soon as you see them—wait for a month and you'll have a whole wall to wash. Don't

forget the light switches (spray the cleaner on a cloth and use it to wipe the switchplates).

3. *Vacuum the entire hall, but just the traffic areas.* Halls are kind of the doormat for the house, so they get it bad. And before you start vacuuming, sweep anything off the edges with a plain old broom.

You should be able to hustle through the hallway in no more than five minutes.

On the other hand, lots of housework originates in the areas just inside and outside the door—the entryways to your house.

1. Hit the doors, ceiling, and railings with your lambs-wool duster.
2. Spot-clean any spills or marks on the walls (people are always going in and out of entryways with their hands full of everything from sandwiches to the new couch).
3. Floors in entryways also get a beating from all of the coming and going. If the entry has a hard floor (tile, ceramic, brick, or wood), sweep, dust mop, or vacuum it well. It probably needs mopping, too, so mop it at the same time you mop the kitchen, which will be the last room you do. If it's a carpet, vacuum with a good beater-bar vac or power wand. Get up all that grit, gravel, and other debris that will otherwise just get pulverized or tracked all over the house.
4. Vacuum your inside (and outside) floor mats (see Chapter 8) well, and keep them vacuumed. They're your lifesavers.

Entryways are highly visible parts of a home, and a little extra time spent here—a total of five to seven minutes—should keep them presentable.

Living Room or Family Room

Avoid the temptation to switch on the TV and collapse a minute. Keep going! Remember the calories you're burning, and all the praise you're going to get from the rest of the household when they notice how nice things look (fat chance, but dreaming always does a lot for our morale).

1. *Straighten up everything first*—furniture, pictures, books, magazines, videos, CDs. It'll make you feel good.
2. *Then dust everything.* Always dust before you vacuum, so the clipped fingernails, bug bodies, and dead leaves will end up where the vacuum will get them. Work from the top down with your lambswool duster, and if there are blinds on the windows be sure to include them. Start with the top of the furniture, too, and work all the way down to the floor on each piece so you don't have to come back to do the low dusting. There's lots of dust within 3 feet of the floor, on the bottoms of the chairs and legs of the furniture. Work your way around the room this way, and then finish off again with the baseboards.
3. *Spot-clean the place; do the carpet too, especially in the area of the TV and entertainment center.* There are lots of food-to-hand and food-to-floor transfers here. (I call it "Orville Redenbacher residue.")
4. *Spot-clean the windows and glass.* (Notice I didn't have you clean the windows in the other rooms—it's best to do that with a squeegee as a whole-house project.) Just touch up any smudges with your spray bottle of glass cleaner and a cloth.
5. *Vacuum the traffic areas.* Remember, the edges and under and behind things don't really have to be done more often than once a month or so. Then set the vacuum outside of the room as a signal that the room is finished.

> What's the best way to clean ashtrays (if they aren't
> so far gone that they need to be soaked in the sink)?
> Dump 'em, spray a couple shots of all-purpose cleaner
> into them, and let them sit for a few minutes. Then come
> back and wipe them out with a dry cleaning cloth.

It shouldn't take more than ten to fifteen minutes to do a living room. If you have a lot of decorations it may take a little longer. But don't get caught up in knickknack renewal or you'll never get out of there.

Kitchen

Save the kitchen until last for several reasons. This is usually the depot for the rest of the house—where we bring things to be cleaned or emptied. The kitchen is the catchall, where we wash out vases and fill bottles, rinse mops, and collect the garbage. Then, too, the kitchen is where we come for breaks and phone calls; if you clean it first, somebody (maybe even you!) is sure to come in there while you're cleaning the rest of the house and dirty it, which is demoralizing. If you get bogged down anywhere, it's probably going to be the kitchen. Better to have that happen at the end of your cleaning than at the beginning. When you do get here:

1. *Dust everything from the top down.* High dusting is critical in the kitchen because all the steam and vapors of cooking will turn dust into grease-cake pretty quickly, and then it'll take a major wash job to get it off. If you keep the kitchen dusted this buildup will have less of a chance to develop. Still, greasy dust collects pretty quickly in places such as the range hood and the tops of the cabinets, so

for much of the kitchen a cloth dampened with dish detergent solution is unquestionably the best duster. The dish soap will give your wiper enough dissolving ability to remove the oil slick. Buff dry with a cleaning cloth right after you damp-wipe so you don't leave streaks or film.

Damp-wiping is a two-step process: clean with a damp cloth, and buff and shine with a clean, dry cloth. This is especially important in kitchen cleaning.

---

2. *Use a lambswool duster to hit the light fixtures and the tops of things* (even those above eye level) first, then the window ledges and moldings. Then with your damp cloth hit the handprints on the fridge and stove front, and the handle area of dishwashers, doors, and drawers. Remember those smudge-collecting small appliances, being especially sure to polish these dry to remove any residue. If you come across any hardened sticky spots, wet them down and let them sit a few minutes while you do something else—you should be able to come back and just whisk them away. This wash/wipe dusting is key to kitchen cleaning. When you do it, save tables and counters for last.

3. *Then straighten things in the kitchen area*—the countertops, tools, and decorations.

4. *Do any dishes and pans that are left around, and wipe the tabletop, chair seats, and counter.* On countertops, start at the back and move canisters and small appliances out of the way. Wipe, and then replace them as you go. Don't worry if any crumbs fall on the floor, because next . . .

5. *You do the floor.* Sweep or dust-mop carefully. On a light day, that should be enough. If kids or company have been around, just toss a shot of all-purpose cleaner into a bucket of water and quickly damp-mop the floor. Any soap residue left will cause dullness, so if you have a super-

shiny vinyl or ceramic tile floor, you might want to rinse with your mop, too, using a little vinegar solution (half a cup of white vinegar per gallon of water) to neutralize it.

6. *While the floor dries, take out the garbage and wash the container.*

All done with the kitchen—in twenty to thirty minutes!

If you come across a stain on a plastic laminate ("Formica") counter, don't start trying to "sand" it off with abrasive cleansers or harsh scrub pads. Once you scratch or mar that slick laminate surface, it'll be porous and hard to clean forever after. If you just get off the worst of the stain with all-purpose cleaner and your white nylon scrub sponge, the rest of it is very likely to eventually fade away with a few days or weeks of ordinary counter wiping. If it doesn't, apply a paste of bleaching cleanser and water and let it dry on there; then remove it carefully so you don't scratch the surface, and the stain should be gone.

Stepping Outside for a Few Minutes a Week . . .

For my first twenty-five years in the professional cleaning business, we were taught (and believed) that the area right inside the door of a place created the first impression, and thus we cleaned lobbies to death. Then one day a perceptive building manager pointed out that the parking lot and exterior entryway were actually the image makers. He was right. We all form a preconception of the inside of a place by what we see and feel going into it.

From then on we cleaned the area directly outside the door as earnestly as the area immediately inside—and with phenomenal results. This is only more true in a home—what do you think when you walk up a sidewalk or onto a porch that resembles an obstacle course of clutter? It sticks in your mind, even if the whole inside of the house is immaculate.

It only takes a few minutes a week to keep the outside nice enough to complement the inside. A little attention to exterior cleaning can also prevent lots of long-range problems inside. Let's take a quick trip around the outside now.

Litter

Maybe it wasn't yours to begin with, but it is now. Litter around the front yard and the lawn is often the first declaration of dirt. Wrappers, cigarette butts, cans, wet envelopes, and newspapers—Mother Nature even chips in some in the form of fallen branches and rotting fruits.

Cure: Make it a practice to pick up litter as soon as you see it, coming and going, and once or twice a month walk around the place with a little sack or box to police under the bushes and against the fence. If you do it right before you take the garbage to the curb, you'll be dressed for it.

Driveway

We often have one vehicle per person, and they all bleed oil and transmission fluid, shed car interior fallout, and drip mud, snow, and road cinders. This not only looks bad on the driveway, but it also can be tracked in and offend the house after it offends the eye.

Cure: Once the driveway is policed by hand or broom, an oil stain on a concrete driveway can be lifted the same as one on a garage floor. Hosing (during the above-freezing months) is a nice finale for the driveway.

Sidewalk

This is the highway to the heart of your house, and all too often it's covered with mud, leaves, twigs, gravel, mashed acorns, leftover ice-melting chemicals, and of course, a few

Problem

STORAGE OUTDOORS. Storage is usually just a polite term for junk left outside and forgotten. It's big, ugly, easy to trip over or get cut on, and encourages termites, rats, and all their relatives.

SCREENS. Screens are often the real culprit when we look up and think, "Gosh, dirty windows!" An amazing amount of dust and dirt (not to mention bird doo and other things) can lodge in all those tiny openings.

DOORS. Doors and the area right around them get hard use every single day—which means scuffs and scrapes as well as plenty of fingerprints and smudges.

PORCHES/STEPS. Porches and steps are such handy places to set things, they end up in a dangerously cluttered condition. They also collect outdoor debris.

WINDOWS. Windows, especially high ones, are often dodged indefinitely because we don't feel like calling in the hook and ladder. And ground-level outside windows get mud-splattered, flyspecked, and cobwebby.

LITTER. Litter makes the place look bad and encourages further littering.

SIDEWALK/DRIVEWAY. A littered, stained walk or driveway gives a bad impression and worsens the track-in problem.

Cure

STORAGE OUTDOORS. The minute you finish that remodeling project, or decide something isn't even good enough to keep in the garage, get the aftermath (the scraps, the old stuff you tore out, etc.) off the premises!.

SCREENS. Clean as described on page 236, or for a quick fix vacuum and then damp-wipe them in place. Don't press hard.

DOORS. Stop ignoring them. Clean your doors and door frames and thresholds, too, every so often as described on page 233. Don't forget the doorknobs!

LITTER. Pick it up as soon as you see it, even if no one you know dropped it there. And at least once a month, put on work gloves and make a delittering run around the whole yard.

PORCHES/STEPS. Declutter daily, clean occasionally as described on page 233, and make sure you have good dirt-catching mats here.

SIDEWALK/DRIVEWAY. Just needs regular attention with a push broom. In warmer months you can just hose them down and follow up with a floor squeegee. (To remove gum, see the next section; for oil stains see page 160.)

WINDOWS. Windows can be done quickly and easily with a squeegee (on an extension pole if they're high windows). If they're really dirty, hose them off first, or use a long-handled scrubber on them.

flattened blobs of chewing gum. Is this how we want to intro-
duce ourselves?

Cure: Get out a sturdy push broom (see the equipment
chart in Chapter 5) and use short strokes to sweep the debris
off to the sides. Or if it's only lightly littered, in the warmer
months you can simply hose it. A clean, newly dried surface
really impresses those walking across it. (That's one of the reasons people are so taken with theme parks like Disneyland, as
I discovered snooping about in the undercorridors with the
maintenance people. They don't sweep every night; they hose
things down.) Then take a floor squeegee and de-water the walk
so the low areas won't have a chance to form scummy puddles
as they dry. **Policing the walk each day as you come and
go takes only seconds and keeps sidewalks looking
smart!** (Pull those weeds in the cracks, too. If they keep coming
back, sprinkle in some salt water—but not so much that it runs
all over.)

Gum on sidewalks, driveways, and paved parking areas
isn't just ugly—it sticks to the bottom of your shoe on a hot
day, too. Go out there when it's cold or at least cool, and you
should be able to chip it right off with a chisel or a hoe. Be
sure to pick up the pieces the minute they're free or you'll
have a worse mess—they'll be tracked everywhere and get on
everything. If it never gets chilly where you live, use a can of
"gum freeze" from a janitorial-supply store. De-Solv-it or dry-
cleaning fluid will take care of any remaining traces. Don't use
solvents on asphalt—they will dissolve it!

As for moss, it not only gives the walk a five-o'clock
shadow—when wet it's slicker than ice! Water alone won't
remove it (it'll just make it grow), and you can't just bleach
it away, either (and you wouldn't want to pour bleach outside anyway). Mix a warm solution of all-purpose cleaner and
spread it generously on the spot. Let it sit awhile (but not
until it evaporates), then scrub and loosen the moss with a
stiff push broom, brush, or hand floor scrubber. Then just

flush it off with a hose (the solution won't hurt the lawn). If a bit remains, go after it again and get it now, while you have everything handy.

Porch

A porch, deck, or sunroom is often a permanent outdoor "junk room." Or if it's a prelude to the entrance we actually use, it gets more traffic and abuse than even the kitchen or bathroom, since it has to contend with both us and the elements.

Cure: Stop using the porch as a place to stash stuff you haven't decided what to do with. *Decide*—and either bring it in or get it out of there for good. Move out all the out-of-season outerwear, dry-rotted boots, and mildewed sneakers. Make sure you have a good floor mat here, too (see Chapter 8). If you have an enclosed porch you have room for a long one— and you should clean it often (just step out the door with the vacuum). Get rid of those cobwebs with a lambswool duster on an extension handle if necessary. Regular sweeping of a porch is the number one way to keep dirt at a distance; swab the floor afterward occasionally with a solution of all-purpose cleaner. Then scrub it lightly with a hand floor scrubber (see the equipment chart in Chapter 5) and rinse. A fresh porch gives a good impression and prevents a lot of inside dirt.

Door Area

Doors and the area around them are about as concentrated an area for dirt collection as they come. We usually carry something with us as we come and go, and as we open and close the door we push, nudge, and lean against it. This often transfers a little of whatever we're carrying, or is on our hands, to the area, especially when we come in from the garden or from fixing the car.

Cure: Most doors—painted or varnished wood, metal, or plastic—can be cleaned the same way. Take a spray bottle of all-purpose cleaner, a thick towel, a white nylon scrub sponge, and a whisk broom, and visit all your outside doors, including the garage door.

1. *Whisk and dust the entire door frame and doorway*—the top and sides will have cobwebs, mashed bugs, and fuzz clinging by static attraction; the bottom (threshold) will have sand and debris in the crevices.

2. *Spray the entire door (especially the area around the knob, and any spots) lightly with the all-purpose cleaner, and while it "simmers" take your soft white nylon sponge and gently hit the black smudges or marks.* Keep the surface wet while you scrub, and don't scrub too hard—remember, the outside surface of the door oxidizes over time and if you scrub that off, the cleaned spots will be a different color.

3. *Wipe the entire surface dry with a towel.* Switch sides as it becomes soiled, so you don't transfer any dirt to already-clean areas.

4. *The doorknob and area around it will be dirtier than it looks, so be sure to clean it.* Then check the doorbell, mailbox, and anything else in the vicinity. The windows and any light fixtures can be cleaned with a spray bottle of glass cleaner. You'll often find tape residue from decorations, messages, and deliveries here—carefully use a little De-Solv-It to remove it chemically, rather than by scrubbing or scraping.

5. *Storm doors get a lot of hard use and abuse, and many of them are made of two of the toughest materials to clean: aluminum and Plexiglas.* Never take any aggressive cleaner or anything sharp to them. Clean them just like the other doors, except be sure to dust or rinse any Plexiglas parts first to remove as much as possible of the dust and grit that can so easily scratch it. Painted aluminum can be sprayed with all-purpose cleaner (or even heavy-duty cleaner if its really grimy), scrubbed with a white nylon scrub sponge after a minute or two, and then polished dry with a

cleaning cloth. Avoid any kind of abrasive because it will damage or degloss the paint. Aluminum that is not anodized (does not have paint fused to the surface) will turn your cloth black everywhere you touch it, and you won't notice much difference in its appearance. Oh well, at least you'll know you have a clean door.

Windows

Any dirt on the upper windows is only noticed from the inside, and they're not usually too bad anyway. But the lower windows are often splattered with bird droppings and mud from rain splashes, and the sills and frames are littered with dead bugs and paint chips. And the window wells are usually full of everything from lost caulk and broken glass to old dog bones and deflated basketballs.

Cure: Clean the high windows like you do inside ones, with a squeegee (just add an extension handle). As for the lower ones, hose them off well first before you apply any cleaner with a window-washing wand. If they're really bad, use a long-handled scrubber (see the equipment chart in Chapter 5) with a white nylon pad to clean them; rinse them well with the hose and squeegee them dry. Then put a bucket down in the window wells and using a gloved hand, fill it up with all the awful stuff you find there.

Screens

These slowly but surely get plugged up, dirty, and damaged, and end up looking seedy.

Cure: If you don't have time to give screens the whole treatment as described on page 115, sweep them lightly with a brush or broom, and damp-wipe them in place (don't push hard or your screens will soon sag!) Replace any that are ripped or bulged.

Outside Storage

The worst of outside cleaning is "stored" stuff, especially anything right up against the house or around the entrance or porch. All those broken bicycles, left-behind tools and containers, piles of rotting firewood, scraps, and half-finished projects don't exactly suggest cleanliness and order.

Cure: Don't ever allow anything to be stored against or around the house. Get rid of it right now. It looks tacky, encourages pests, and injures people as well as siding. If it isn't worth storing in a garage, barn, or shed, it probably isn't worth keeping. Pile it up by the back fence and cover it with a tarp if you must, but keep loose stuff away from the house—all of it!

Garage

Even if you're actually able to get your car(s) into your garage, you probably have to squeeze it in carefully, past all of the junk fitted in around it.

1. *You always start in a garage by dejunking it.* This is a regular ongoing process, not a once-a-year spring garage sale surge. You go to the garage for some reason almost every day, passing right by all this stuff. So take one or two things with you on each trip and keep the junk controlled.

2. *Pick up all the scattered tools and sports equipment and hang them up.* If you've done this twenty-seven times this month already, it's time to take a break. Get some of those wall-hung tool organizers and lick the problem once and for all.

3. *Whisk off (don't dust) any horizontal surfaces such as tables, cabinets, and shelves with one of those counter or foxtail brushes.* You may find it hard to locate the horizontal surfaces—so dejunk some more and do it anyway.

4. *Treat the shop area the same as the kids' room.* Trash the trash, remove anything deadly, and round up the rest. Then pile it neatly in the owner's territory.

5. *Put all that broken stuff* (the "I'm going-to-fix-it-someday" junk) in a sturdy box and pray for its deliverance. (Or get rid of all the things that will never actually be fixed and take time out next weekend to fix the few that are left).

6. *Get out your push broom* (if you have a garage you ought to have one!) and sweep the floor. Sweep around the oil drips; don't push the broom through them.

7. *As for the oil drips, sprinkle some sawdust or kitty litter on them, pour a little paint thinner on, and mix well.* Then cover the spot or spots with some plastic wrap or a damp rag for a few hours. You've just created what we call a "poultice." It will suck up the oil and after it's done its dirty work you can sweep it away into the trash. If any stain remains it can usually be removed by scrubbing with a stiff brush and a solution of ordinary powdered laundry detergent and water.

Chapter Seventeen

Your Reward:
There Is Life After Housework!

Well, that's it. We've covered enough aspects of housework to provide a fresh, more positive view of the subject. And until a robot is developed that can be programmed to do your housework for you, you'll find the methods and equipment outlined in the foregoing chapters to be the next best thing for getting the most work done in the least amount of time.

Just remember that the home is the most sacred and exciting place on the face of the earth. For anyone to pronounce that caring for a home is a hardship, a drag, and a bore is only to admit a lack of imagination. Those who clean and care for a house, whether on a full-time basis or in addition to another career, can get great satisfaction from it.

Remember, though, that a house is to live in, not live for. Cleanliness is important, but it should never become all-important. There is merit in being meticulous, in adding that extra touch of excellence to your efforts, but there is also room for caution here: Our zeal to achieve superior results can become slavish devotion to meaningless detail.

Homes are more than showcases and status symbols. Your home is the background against which your life is lived, your retreat from the world's buffetings. Why direct all your efforts toward impressing society? There's great fun and satisfaction in giving yourself to your surroundings, and in making your home a pleasing reflection of your personality and interests. People will enjoy coming to your house, not because of its impressive trappings and expensive adornments, but because so much of *you* is there.

Personal freedom is life's real reward. Housework is an important and worthwhile endeavor, but the less of your life it requires, the more will be available for other pursuits that add dimension and joy and meaning to living.

Why Do We Mind the Time Spent Cleaning?

The whole thrust of humankind is to do, build, or create something that will last forever—be it a family, a reputation, a building, a poem, or a pyramid. We want something that will last, maybe for thousands or tens of thousands of years, to testify to our lives of hard work and inspiration. . . .

And then there is housework—especially cleaning. We spend many (including some of the best) hours of our life making something beautiful and presentable—a glossy floor or sparkling windows, a dust-free curio cabinet or lint-free living-room rug—then a few more hours or a few days and little appreciation later it's gone, and we're right back where we began. We size it all up, the thirty or forty tasks that we do over and over each day or week, and think, "I should look forward to doing *this*?" Yes, and here's why: When it seems you've been unjustly stuck with cleaning up behind someone or something, think of this. Great meals, great buildings, great novels, bumper crops, and crown jewels all make some dust or mess in getting the job done. Cleaning it up is not only worthwhile, it's actually part and parcel of the end result. Cleaning affects the quality of life much more than parties, entertainments, and vacations, and look at all the effort and money we pour into them. So just think as you clean up, "This is not the aftermath, but the launch. . . . I'm preparing for the liftoff of great things."

When you think of the impact, the accomplishments of the "clean" you've created in your life, and when you focus on the end result, cleaning feels good and necessary and even noble.

Pulpit, pedestal, or poetry cannot enrich the lives of others like a clean, happy, well-organized home life can. Humankind needs examples of order and confidence, and both of these virtues can be superbly exemplified in the home.

Children and grownups, too, need order in their lives. A feeling of contentment, comfort, and wellbeing grows out of neatness and order, not clutter and chaos. Self-esteem and achievement germinate in a quality environment, and no environment is more influential than the home. Our home atmosphere has a great influence on all of us—it can affect lives far more than any movie star, president, or professor. The spirit of our home can touch and change not only all those who enter and all who live there, but our own close personal relationships as well. It can make us irresistible as people— someone not just to be needed, but loved and appreciated.

The home is the power lever of the world, and *you* control it.

You can save about 75 percent of the time, tools, and money you spend on cleaning if you use the methods and materials the professionals do, as I have explained in these pages. If you are not experiencing exhilaration from your role as a home cleaner, it may be because your family has so much emotional and physical clutter that they can't reach you or one another to give love and appreciation. There is no greater goal or achievement on the face of the earth than the opportunity to love and in turn be loved. Thrashing around in the clutter of a home too often thwarts the opportunity to achieve this. Skilled, efficient care of a decluttered home will take fewer hours, fewer supplies, fewer repairs, will prevent tension, and will give us more room and a greater capacity to grow into new friendships and experiences. First things first. *Living* is life . . . and we want to have as much of it as possible after housework!

Get Those Other Hands to Help!

When looking for ways to find life after housework, remember that your resources include your family's ability to pick up after themselves and otherwise help out. If they're old enough to mess up, they're old enough to clean up.

Millions of readers have gotten quite a chuckle from the observations in Chapter 4 on getting help from the rest of the family, and this is probably still the case in the majority of homes across the country—but it's a slowly shrinking majority. I give a standing ovation to those homes where everyone takes care of him- or herself and is not dependent on Mom to pick up and take care of everything. **Cleaning isn't women's work, it's the work of those who created the need for it,** and I promise you I won't rest until that truth is taught to all and practiced by most.

It's not a woman's job to clean, but tradition takes time to change. What you used to see as the thankless chores of housework might well be some of your greatest teaching moments. Remember the potential lesson to be taught the next time . . .

- You spend four hours preparing a lovely family dinner and end up with only a 3-foot stack of dirty dishes.
- You spend sixteen hours sewing a satin drill team costume and are rewarded with a whimper about the hemline.
- You proudly present a fat, tidy row of freshly washed and dried shirts to your spouse, and he or she says, "Where's my blue one?"
- You are on duty around the clock nursing the family through a siege of the flu, yet when it's your turn to collapse into a sickbed, there's not a soul around to nurse you.
- You know the kids are home by the trail of coats and books left in their wake or by the jam and peanut butter and empty glasses covering the counter.

Remember, if you don't teach them, who will? Help yourself out; give cleaning books (or a copy of *HELP! Around the House: A Mother's Guide to Getting the Family to Pitch In and Clean Up* to the groom, the athlete, the son, the engineer, the father. It may take a while, but you watch: It will work. I see a change coming.

There is *Life After Housework!*

Index

About the Author

The man who went door to door cleaning houses to work his way through college, more than fifty years later, is now the head of one of the nation's leading professional cleaning companies. His company, Varsity Contractors, is now a multimillion-dollar operation cleaning homes and businesses across the country.

Don Aslett isn't just America's #1 Cleaning Expert, he's everyone's favorite cleaner. For more than two decades now he's been teaching people how to clean faster and better, and even more amazing, keeping them smiling all the while.

He burst on the national scene in 1981 with the first edition of this book, a book that became an instant bestseller and is now almost a household word. For the first time ever, it brought the tools and techniques of the professionals to the aid of the home cleaner. And its appreciation of the often underrated value of homemaking won him the hearts of homemakers everywhere.

Don has written more than two dozen equally popular books since, bringing his refreshingly down-to-earth and original approach not only to cleaning, but also to decluttering, personal organization, self-help, and how to better yourself in business. His books are perennial bestsellers—they've sold more than 3 million copies to date—and they've been featured by major books clubs and translated into many other languages.

Don is also active in civic, church, and youth groups such as the Boy Scouts. He and his wife Barbara have six children and divide their time between their ranch in McCammon, Idaho, and their winter home in Kauai, Hawaii.

Acknowledgments

Like housework, a book is not just one person's doing. The author puts all his ideas and energy into it, but a fine finished volume like this is the work of a team.

People who did a lot to make a success of the earlier editions of this book include: *Gladys Allen*, a highly organized mother of many, dejunking engineer, and entertainer; attorney *John Preston Creer; Ernest Garrett;* and *Clark Carlile,* my college speech teacher (and a successful publisher himself), who encouraged me never to lose my humor and "enthusiastic" style of expressing myself. *Mark Lloyd Browning* and *Jim Doles,* longtime colleagues and executives of Varsity Contractors, rendered expert technical assistance and feedback. *Budge Wallis,* of F + W Publications, was one of my first and best publishing champions. *Judith Holmes Clarke* and *Craig LaGory* provided illustrations and design that did much to bring earlier editions of this book to life.

For the handsome new look and help with the updating of this latest edition we must thank Bridget Brace, Paula Munier, Gary Krebs, and Holly Curtis of Adams Media, as well as Tad Herr, and Jim Hunt.

And through all of its editions, this now cleaning classic has had the assistance of Carol Cartaino, the all-time best editor in the world, and Tobi Flynn, the woman who makes it all happen.